GRAY & COLUMBIA'S RIVER

CAPTAIN ROBERT GRAY

Joean K. Fransen (signature)

GRAY & COLUMBIA'S RIVER

Joean K. Fransen

BINFORD & MORT PUBLISHING
Portland, Oregon

THIS BOOK IS DEDICATED TO W.O.

TWO R'S, TWO F'S AND CINDY

THE NATIVES BROUGHT
BERRIES TO THE CREW TO
HELP RELIEVE THOSE ILL
WITH SCURVY.

THE SEA OTTER, UNIQUE
TO THE PACIFIC, WAS
BEING SOUGHT WORLD-
WIDE FOR IT'S FINE,
SOFT FUR.

**THE INDIANS
DESIRED THESE SMALL
COPPER SQUARES
CALLED "CHIPOKS"
IN TRADE FOR THE SEA
OTTER PELTS.**

This book is the fulfillment of a promise to the students and staff of Captain Robert Gray School situated at the mouth of the Columbia River, who searched in vain for a book telling the Captain Robert Gray story.

Gray is important in American history as his entrance into the long sought River of the West gave the United States a claim to the Oregon Country; the land that eventually became the states of Oregon, Washington, Idaho and parts of Montana and Wyoming. This intrepid explorer, the great-grandson of Sir Edward Gray who arrived at Plymouth, Massachusetts in 1641; reaffirmed the expanse of the 1621 colonial charter issued by the King of England, granting the Plymouth Company land from the 40th to the 48th parallel from "sea to sea."

Robert Gray was the first American to circumnavigate the globe on an American vessel flying the American flag. Only part of Volume I and an extract from Volume II remain from Gray's logs of his two voyages to the Pacific Northwest. Gray did not leave a diary, nor did he write his memoirs. His terse

**ALL THE SHIP'S IRON
THAT COULD BE SPARED
WAS HAMMERED INTO
CHISELS TO BE TRADED
FOR THE PELTS.**

letters to Kendrick and the Boston ship-owners were very business-like. He left few words of his own on which to judge him but his actions truly speak loudly of his inner character.

The partial logs and narratives of Robert Haswell, John Hoskins, and John Boit, seamen who sailed on the *Lady Washington* and the *Columbia Rediviva*, give clues to Gray's disposition. The writings of Frederick W. Howay, Samuel Eliot Morison, Warren L. Cook, Dorothy O. Johansen, Edmund S. Meaney, and John R. Jewett, as well as notable histories and historians of the area and the times, have aided in the research.

To the bare bones of a daily account one may add a careful, yet lively, existence to the people of the past; giving them the flesh of humanity, the muscle of courage, and the heart of a patriot. A thin thread of imagination has been woven into the history, facts, and dates to make this two-hundred-year-old-event and Captain Robert Gray's actions come alive for today's reader.

**1787 AND 1788 FIRST VOYAGE - IN THE
PACIFIC - OFF SOUTH AMERICA.**

Three small boys were playing around the local dock in the bay near the Puritan settlement of Tiverton. It was late afternoon in 1763. Two of the boys were laughing and taunting the third, who had just revealed his most private dream: what he had wanted to do when he grew up.

"He wants to sail around the world!" scoffed a shrill voice.

"Robert Gray thinks he can be another Columbus!" jeered the skinny one.

"He says he wants to explore and discover new

lands!" added the first eight year old as he scuffed his feet through the world map of oceans and continents Robert had drawn in the sand.

"Robert-Gray-wants-to-be-an-ex-plor-er," the two chanted in unison.

"Sure, and then he can go to the moon," was the final insult as the two ran off toward the cluster of houses set back from the beach, leaving the dreamer to consider his incomplete world.

In his dream, laughter and hoots became unbearably louder and louder. Robert tossed and turned, wrestling with the painful scene. Frustration and rage made him lash out. The dream, the memory, made him wake up thrashing on his bunk in the warm cabin.

The taunts and jeers faded into the thirsty bleats of Nancy, the ship's goat. Moonlight skipped back and forth as Robert began to recognize his surroundings. He was that boy long ago. He was the boy in the dream who wanted to sail around the world and be an explorer. Now twenty-five years later, he was a man on a round-the-world voyage adventure.

His small sailing vessel was one-half of the first American expedition journeying to enter the fur trade with China. He was the captain of the sixty-foot sloop, *Lady Washington* out of Boston. It had been ten months since he and his crew of God-and-devil-fearing New Englanders had glided silently past Boston Light, outbound for Nootka Sound, a dot on the uncharted Northwest Pacific coast.

The *Lady* was rocking gently in the night as she plowed slowly north in the South Pacific, slowed by the build-up of barnacles and marine life attached to her wooden hull.

Robert was worried about his crew. The merciless sun had been beating down for weeks. The water rations were so low there was scant moisture in the men's bodies. The mate ordered the deck sloshed with sea water to prevent the planks from cracking open but this aggravated the salt-water sores on the parched hands and feet of the miserable crew. There was no wood onboard to use for cooking the live animals and the salt pork was so harsh in the sailors' dehydrated stomachs it made them retch when they tried to eat it.

No rain had fallen into the waiting canvas stretched to the large empty water barrels. Night-time brought some relief, but during the day there was no respite from the heat, certainly not in the dark, windowless, cramped quarters below deck.

Robert was born with the desire for world-wide adventure. He had grown up in Tiverton, Rhode Island on the banks of Narranganset Bay, watching every kind of sailing vessel, from the small packets that crisscrossed the sheltered inland waters carrying passengers, freight, and mail to the large ships that docked at the long wharfs bringing passengers and cargo from England, mainland Europe, and the Mediterranean.

Robert knew he wanted to be a deep-water sailor, no coaster command for him!

For years explorers had been seeking a Northwest Passage: a waterway across North America to shorten the route to the Orient. Gray was born to tales of these adventurers. In fact, in 1744 the English Parliament had offered the incredible sum of a £20,000 reward for the first Englishman to sail through this passage. Captain James Cook, the famous English explorer, had not found such a route across North America, however, his third voyage to the

Pacific brought back the news of the sea otter trade with China. The magnificent furs of this North Pacific mammal were in high demand in China.

Boston vessels sailing to the Orient around Africa, by the Cape of Good Hope, had met great success in disposing of the exotic Oriental goods they brought back. The problem the Americans had was in finding a cargo that would be in demand in China.

The dream reminded Robert of his desire to search for the Northwest Passage. Unfortunately he had not counted on the quarreling and stalling of Captain John Kendrick on the command vessel, the *Columbia Rediviva*, the other vessel in the expedition. Robert had managed not to become involved in the rows Kendrick had with his crew members. However, at the very first stop in the Cape Verdes, he watched regretfully as the chief officer on the *Columbia*, and the expedition's doctor, both went ashore because of continuing dissatisfaction with Kendrick. As he was leaving the *Columbia*, the chief warned those still aboard that Kendrick's disagreeable, antagonistic command would continue.

At that stop, in the Cape Verdes, Robert and the

Lady Washington fidgeted for forty-one long days waiting for Kendrick to complete filling the water casks on the *Columbia,* a chore that should have taken about five days.

Even though Robert was impatient to continue the voyage, he considered himself fortunate, however, for while they waited for "Cap'n Jack" Kendrick to re-stow his eighty foot command ship, Robert signed on the native black boy, Marcus Lopez, with his nanny goat. Marcus proved to be an eager, helpful cabin boy and his goat's milk was a welcome daily addition to tea. The crew named her Nancy.

Between the gales and boisterous weather of the passage to the Falklands, Robert, the experienced seaman who could close his eyes anytime and easily "see" and identify the constellations of the northern sky, had watched the night-time darkness closely. He compared new sightings to his celestial charts and carefully noted his first glimpse of the Southern Cross.

Eventually, the two ship expedition made the Falkland Islands off the tip of South America. Here, friction on the *Columbia* surfaced again. When the second officer, Robert Haswell, attempted to desert on these bleak and uninhabited islands, Kendrick reluctantly agreed to allow the young officer to transfer to the *Lady Washington*. Robert's crew, on the *Lady Washington*, then swelled to number ten men.

While in the Falklands, again Kendrick persisted in mindless delays. Finally, when the officers and crews became almost mutinous, he was forced to give the order to sail. They set out to best Cape Horn, the southern most point of the Americas. It was March, the most turbulent sailing month of the year.

Whenever Robert thought of that leg of the voyage, his disgust with Kendrick also returned. All of the unnecessary delays had caused Kendrick to risk the expedition in the raging March weather. For some time both vessels survived the mountainous waves crashing over their decks, the violent winds that shredded the sails, the penetrating, numbing cold, and even the silently drifting peaks and pillars of ice islands.

Regretfully, a dreadful catastrophe appeared to

have happened one month into the rounding. On April 1st, during one of the un-ending violent gales, with winds carrying hail, sleet, and snow, the *Columbia Rediviva*, Captain Kendrick, and crew, disappeared down into the trough of a great grey-beard of a wave. No one saw it reappear. Now, almost two months later, as the *Lady Washington* neared the Pacific equator, there was still no sign of the command ship. Was it a cruel April Fool's joke?

AUGUST 16, 1788 - FIRST STOP

AT MURDERER'S HARBOR.

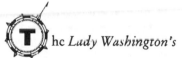 he *Lady Washington's*

crew could guess their Captain was already at sea when

some of them were born. His admirers would jok-

ingly boast that Gray had learned the ropes at the

same time he was cutting his teeth, further, that he

got into trouble with the schoolmaster for wrangling

short trips with skipper-friends across Narraganset

Bay, when he should have been studying his primer.

In truth, his early life at sea as a cabin boy had lasted

only until he had grown old enough and strong enough

to sing out the chanteys and pull his weight with his

mates in the rigging. He knew the sailor's life both

as one of the lads and as an officer. He used his authority carefully. He was fair and just, but he could order a flogging when necessary

When the rains finally came and with them good winds to carry the small vessel smartly across the equator and into northern latitudes, Robert looked up at stars in the night sky and welcomed familiar friends from his childhood.

Robert felt justifiable satisfaction in the fact that he had not been turned back rounding the Horn. Others had. Others had been lost.

Robert would learn later that seagoing men stood in awe of him when they learned that at the same time he was making this successful passage around the Horn in the small sloop the *Lady Washington,* the determined Englishman and expert sailor, Captain William Bligh on *The Bounty,* was challenging the same hazardous elements of cold, wind, and waves on his voyage around the Horn bound for Tahiti. Bligh battled the brutal seas and frigid weather until severe damage to his ship and casualties among the crew forced him to turn back.

Gray re-read Kendrick's orders (should they become separated) and he was confident he would be able to complete the expedition to the satisfaction of the owners.

He rejoiced in having avoided cannibals on uncharted South Pacific islands, but now his immediate concern was to get relief for the crew members afflicted with scurvy, the dietary disease that regularly struck sailors on long sea voyages. Some of the crew found they could not eat because of swollen mouths and gums. Weakness and extreme pain in their arms and legs kept others in their bunks.

Since late in the 1500s when the bold Englishman, Drake, had raided Spanish holdings on both sides of South America, the Spanish maintained a vigilant policy of capturing any vessels found in their waters. For this reason Robert had set the *Lady's* course far out to sea. He reckoned they should be north of Spanish holdings soon. Then they could get ashore for fresh greens, mullen and wild celery, and fresh water for the ailing crew.

As soon as they reached 40° N, Robert turned

toward the continent. On August 2, 1788, the look-out sighted the coast of Sir Francis Drake's "New Albion." The expedition was now on the west coast of the North American continent, at about the same latitude as Robert's birthplace on the eastern coast: Tiverton, Rhode Island. Gales and on-shore winds prevented an exchange with the first two canoes of Native Americans that came off. Finally, in mid-August, after five and one-half months at sea, Robert guided the *Lady Washington* into a small bay at about 44° N on the northwest coast of America. Curious visitors from the Indian village on the shore were lured close to the sloop with gifts of buttons and trinkets. In return, the natives brought berries and boiled crab, both of which helped to relieve those ill with scurvy.

Trading for furs eventually began. Since the Americans did not have the sheets of copper the Indians desired, the first few luxurious sea otter pelts were eventually purchased for knives and axes.

The Indians, about two at a time, were allowed to roam about the open deck. Robert reminded the crew of warnings by previous traders regarding the natives' petty thievery. The visitors kept their weapons always ready to strike, but seemed to relax as they studied the live animals aboard, and watched with wonder as the goat, Nancy, frisked and gamboled about the deck.

For the first time since the Falklands, crews were cautiously sent ashore. Wood was close at hand, but only one party was sent for fresh water since the creek was beyond the protection of the sloop's guns.

The next day dawned calm; no breeze to fill the sails, and there also was a strong in-coming tide. Both of these conditions kept the *Lady* in the harbor. As there had been no incidents and those with scurvy would greatly benefit from going ashore to gather and eat wild greens, Robert permitted two officers, Coolidge and Haswell, to go ashore with the sick. A crew, including the cabin boy, Marcus, went along to cut grass for the animals aboard.

The two officers visited the Indian village and mingled with the natives without incident. Haswell related that the men were clothed in animal skins and the women wore a short skirt of straw. The Yanks had sampled dried salmon and fruit, but declined the unnamed items floating in fish oil.

The two were being given a vividly frightening demonstration believed to be a war dance when shouts broke out down at the water's edge. The officers ran quickly to investigate - only to discover that an Indian had seized Marcus' unattended cutlass and had run into the brush with it. Without considering the danger, Marcus had followed him and was calling for help. Other members of the crew nearby followed the two through the undergrowth until they came upon Marcus struggling with the Indian. He pleaded for help to subdue the thief, but as they watched, horrified, Marcus fell victim to the merciless spears and arrows of the steadily growing circle of hostile Indians.

The Americans on shore realized they were inadequately armed and hopelessly outnumbered. They drew their pistols, but were forced to flee before a following rain of arrows and spears. Several of them were injured, one bleeding badly, as they scrambled for the boat.

Fortunately, the guns on the sloop's deck turned back the canoes of pursuing, hooting natives.

That night Robert did not need to order the terrified crew to keep a careful watch. The Indians' beach fires were plainly visible and their whoops and howls carried easily across the water of the small harbor; but no canoes came off.

The next morning was Sunday. Again, the calm and the flood tide held the *Lady* bar-bound. The watch reported the only activity of the day when a large war canoe was seen at some distance leaving the harbor.

Monday morning brought further weather complications; dense fog had settled in. The crew on the helpless sloop became extremely anxious and especially attentive to any muffled sounds in the murkiness. Would the fog and surf cover the sounds of the *Lady's* creaking planking and gear? Could the Indians on nearby hills see the mast standing above the fog? Were the Indians nearby on the beach, or gathering outside the bar?

Suddenly, out of the fog, three large war canoes silently appeared. Each was loaded with about thirty warriors, armed with spears and bent bows, advancing warlike toward the sloop. They did not give way to warning shouts.

The gunners aboard began to sweat in the dawn dampness. At the last possible moment Robert gave the order to fire. Only when the swivel guns were discharged in their direction did the canoes quickly turn and paddle back into the fog.

The morning dragged on. Finally, around noon, the weather cleared and a light breeze picked up. Robert quickly gave the order and the eager crew sprang to action. A most welcome wind filled the sails and the sloop was carried safely out into the open sea.

Later, Mate Haswell explained to the Captain that there had been no possibility of returning with the body of the slain cabin boy. Robert reasoned: Marcus could have given up the knife, but his sense of justice must have forced him to charge after the Indian. In the end he lost his life and risked the safety of the expedition. Robert could not afford to lose crew members over equipment. He was not sailing in the Mediterranean where he could sign on a man at the next port. He ordered that deck tools, clothing, and small navigational aids must be secured at all times.

Dismayed by the clash with the natives and the death of the cabin boy, Robert turned to the charts and appropriately named the place Murderers' Harbor.

Since it was their first stop on the northwest coast, some of the crew began to speculate about the possibility of the River of the West emptying into the small bay. Perhaps Robert searched mentally through his experiences in harbors fed by great rivers. Did he conclude the influx of fresh water here would need to be much greater to indicate the drainage of a large part of the western continent?

The sound of Nancy's plaintive bleating for Marcus made the crew sad, but Robert ordered the *Lady Washington* to continue north. He wondered privately if the rumored Pacific cannibals would be at the next stop.

SEPTEMBER 16, 1788 ARRIVAL AT

NOOTKA SOUND - ENGLISH

FUR TRADERS - KENDRICK'S

ARRIVAL.

The Indian's obvious distrust of the whites troubled Robert. His officers noted that Captain Gray had not sought revenge by firing on the village, as perhaps others had. The Americans would abide by their government's order, commanding only fair treatment in trading.

The Captain expected the natives to come aboard during future trading and he feared that their well-known pilfering could lead to other serious incidents. Recognizing his vessel's vulnerability when anchored near well populated villages, Robert further announced that no reprisals would be made for any items taken.

Leaving Murderers' Harbor, the *Lady* continued north in contrary, unpleasant weather, keeping
a close watch for another harbor. More than once,
Robert muttered, "Blast this rain and fog," as he caught
only a glimpse of the high forbidding coastal headlands. He was kept busy noting on the charts the
rocks and reefs that dotted the coast waters.

But even more disheartening than the weather
and the dangerous waters, was the fact that the Indians demanded copper in trade for furs. They showed
the Yanks the "chipoks" they desired; the treasured
two or three inch squares of hammered copper. Few
trades could be made for the sea otter furs offered,
as the natives scorned the trade goods the Yanks had
brought. Everyone aboard was melancholy as they
watched the canoes that came to trade, laden with
the dense beautiful pelts, return to the beach un-
touched.

Once the sloop had plowed north past 45° N,
Robert hardly needed to order a careful watch. The
crew knew the widely circulated story of the 1592
voyage told by the old Greek pilot, Juan de Fuca.
He declared he had sailed into and explored a wide

strait that penetrated the northwest coast of America between 47° and 48° N latitude. Not many believed it passed shores lined with gold, silver, and pearls and ended in the mythical Sea of the North, but, suppose the Spanish had suppressed publication of the discovery of a great waterway to keep other nations away? To a man, the crew on this vessel wanted to pursue the old legend.

As they continued north, still headed for Nootka Sound at 49° 32' N, a peaceful exchange with the natives in sleek efficient whaling canoes took place at 47° 28' N. Fish and berries were welcome but these people had few furs to trade.

Snow peaks were sighted ashore. Foggy, disagreeable weather persisted.

On August 26, 1788, Robert saw the low coastal land give way. Shortly after they passed the 48° N latitude, he caught sight of an unmistakable opening of sea water penetrating the coast. The muscles around his chest became so tight that he could not take a breath.

It had to be the Juan de Fuca Strait!

The tars cheered and jumped about as they too

strained their eyes in the fog to view the fabled opening. For years sailors had argued about the story.

As for a great discovery, Robert realized the sighting had been too easy. He could not possibly be the first mariner to verify Juan de Fuca's claim. There had been reports of far too many fur traders on this coast in the past few years. Still, it was exciting! One could wonder about the length of it. How far it penetrated into the continent? And Robert's private quest: what great river spilled into it? Was it the end of the Northwest Passage?

There were many more questions, but for now Robert knew he would need copper for next summer's trading season. That was the trade goods the natives demanded.

Robert was determined. He had only discouraging results trying to trade beads and trinkets for furs. It was late August in 1788. He knew he could easily make China, meet with the representatives of the owners, get the copper sheets, and return to the coast in time for the 1789 summer's trading season.

The *Lady* must continue north to find Nootka Sound. There they could refresh the sick, make repairs, and gather provisions to continue the voyage to China.

Two days later, on a calm afternoon as the sloop skirted the northwest edge of the continent, the Americans were surprised by a singing flotilla of three canoes, each containing about fifteen young natives. The Yanks ringed the deck as they watched the natives dip their oars to a pleasing lively rhythm and circle the sloop three times. They sang and stroked and then marked the serenade with a smart routine of paddles pointed aft then forward, accented with shouts and calls. At the conclusion the chief came aboard.

The younger crew members had to take refuge behind barrels and gear on the deck to hide their laughter as a pompous little man clambered over the rail on short, misshapen legs. They watched this ludicrous figure as he scuttled about like a circus clown; knees bent and carefully placing one inward-turned foot after the other. He was dressed unbelievably in a full suit of Englishman's clothes. The jacket fit well enough, as his arms and shoulders were well devel-

"CHIEF MACQUINNA" COURTESY OF THE VANCOUVER PUBLIC LIBRARY - NEG# 54727

THE NATIVES WORE
SKINS OR SHORT
GARMENTS OF WOVEN
CEDAR BARK,
ANIMAL WOOL,
OR HAIR.
THEY DID NOT
WEAR SHOES, BUT
A WOVEN CEDAR
BARK CONICAL
HAT WAS WORN
TO SHED THE
RAIN.

oped; but the mismatched row of brass buttons marching down the jacket front were buttoned askew, and the ruffled shirtwaist was missing. The drastically cropped pantaloons flapped and fluttered over his deformed ankles and sprawling feet.

He wore a tooth and fur necklace and from each ear a long white bead hung on a leather thong.

This shoeless figure with garish red and black face paint, topped with a conical woven hat, and escorted by near naked braves may have appeared comical, but Robert thought there was no humor in the underlying message the chief brought. He spoke of English fur traders: Barkley, Hannah, Meares, and Duncan. Meares had given him the clothes. If Robert understood what was implied, the English were already well established in the northwest fur trade.

These Indians had many fine furs to trade for muskets or copper. But as Robert had neither, no muskets to spare and no copper, no bargains could be struck. The company departed, again singing an enjoyable tune.

Hurrying on, within days the *Lady Washington* stood off the entrance to Nootka Sound.

A ship's small boat came off. It was the English traders, John Meares and William Douglas, offering to pilot the Americans across the bar into Nootka Sound.

Kendrick was not there.

As would be expected in this lonely outpost, the newcomers were at some disadvantage to the two veteran English fur traders. The Yanks were immediately warned of the fierce Indian tribe located here, which had only very recently moved to their winter village at a more protected inland site on the sound.

The Englishmen also protested how scant the fur trade had become.

They urged Robert and his crew to abandon their quest, elaborating on the dangers of sailing in the uncharted waters.

Robert noted, however, that Meares had a crew busily completing a small schooner to use in the next season of coastal fur trading.

Eventually the Englishmen's sea-stories, threats, and tall tales were sorted out and both parties amicably exchanged supplies and assistance with repairs.

The summer fur-gathering season being over, the English captains began to prepare their vessels to sail. However, they made one final excursion to the Indians' inland village. The Americans were shocked to learn the Englishmen forcefully took whatever food or supplies they chose from the helpless natives.

Meares planned to leave soon, on his vessel the *Felice Adventurer* to deliver furs to Macau; the ancient, fabled, trading center in China.

The other two English captains: Douglas on the *Iphigenia* and Funter on the just launched *Northwest America,* planned to winter on the mid-Pacific islands the great English explorer Captain James Cook had named the Sandwich Islands. As the traders stood shivering on the overcast, damp north coast, the Englishmen described in detail the warm, sandy beaches, soft tropical breezes, and the friendly native-Hawaiians waiting there.

Robert knew there was a possibility that Kendrick and the *Columbia* were safe in some harbor on the vast expanse of the west coast of the Americas. It might be months before all the questions would be answered concerning them. "Kendrick's probably held at anchor some place by his own indecision to leave," Robert accused mentally. Robert did not plan to wait; he decided to sail to China. He ordered the crew to prepare for a voyage across the Pacific to get copper for trade with the natives.

The promise of that stop in the mid-Pacific to enjoy the legendary warmth of the Sandwich Islands made the *Lady's* crew work with good will. The sick drank the bitter spruce tea and ate greens regularly to regain their health as soon as possible. Robert calculated they would be ready to leave in a little over a week, as the repairs had been made and the wooding and watering would soon be complete.

September 23, 1788 Kendrick arrived. Two of the *Columbia's* crew had perished from scurvy. The rest were in an advanced stage. Robert quickly ordered all hands to provide greens and other refreshments to aid in their recovery.

The Englishmen sailed away to warm lands and friendly anchorage.

**THE WINTER OF 1788 AND 1789 -
CHISELS - CHRISTMAS - FIRE ON
THE COLUMBIA REDIVIVA.**

he *Columbia* had sur-
vived the ordeal of rounding the Horn but heavy gales
further disabled both the vessel and crew. By late
May the battered *Columbia* was off the coast of South
America at about 34° S. Torn between a certain grave
in the blue salt water of the South Pacific and the risk
of capture by the Spanish, Kendrick chose to throw
his pitiful group on the mercy of the governor of the
lonely Spanish island Juan Fernandez. Governor
Gonzalez had been their savior. He allowed the Yanks
to enter the harbor. The needed supplies were pro-

vided by the Spanish and soon repairs were begun. After a stay of about seventeen days, the *Columbia* departed without incident.

Much to the disappointment of Robert and his crew, the arrival of Kendrick meant they now were forced to await Kendrick's orders.

Predictably, Kendrick ordered both vessels to stay in the harbor to winter in the small cove in Nootka Sound.

Kendrick knew Robert chafed under his laggard command. He watched very carefully to see that his authority was not challenged.

There was no open disagreement.

Robert was not ready to suffer the consequences of mutiny, but he could not accept wasting the winter on the northwest coast and be forced to miss the next summer's trading season for a lack of trading goods. He wanted trade goods to be available as early as possible the next spring. As Kendrick would not permit the *Lady Washington* to use the time during the winter months to sail to China for the small squares of copper demanded by the Indians, Robert had thought of one trade goods possibility. In his contacts with the natives as he had come up the coast, he had noticed they did not have iron tools. They might trade furs for chisels.

The sloop's smith hammered out a few simple one-inch wide, sharpened hand tools and Robert cleverly managed to offer one in trade while Kendrick was watching. It got the desired results. Kendrick ordered all the iron that could be spared to be worked into chisels for trade.

As soon as the abusive "King's men" had left, the formerly terrorized Indians began friendly relations with the Americans they called "Boston men." They provided fish, roots, and venison, in trade for trinkets from the sloop's trade goods.

The Commander ordered the *Lady Washington*, a single masted sloop, modified into a two masted square-rigged brig. Work was begun and spars cut before Kendrick discovered he did not have sails and line enough to accommodate the change. He also ordered a house built on shore, but it was abandoned before completion.

On October 1, 1788, the anniversary of the vessels departure from the eastern side of the continent, the Captains and crews eagerly laid work aside. In spite of the rainy, disagreeable weather, a thirteen gun salute was fired at noon to honor the Thirteen States. The crews spent the day at leisure and the officers dined on board the *Columbia.*

The ship's chimney on the deck of the *Lady Washington* needed to be replaced. The simple fireplace the crew completed was enclosed in a snug building. Robert's crew had hot meals and a warm shelter here when the cold winter brought frost and snow.

As time permitted, Robert directed his crew in building a bulwark around the deck of the *Lady* to provide protection from high waves and also for a better defense in case of a native attack and attempt to board.

Even though he had a good brass stove aboard, Kendrick, too, decided to build a chimney on the *Columbia.* His tottering brick smokestack with its irregular, gaping appearance invited bets on how long it would last.

As winter set in, the wet dense forests did not

invite exploration. However, Haswell and some of the others went deer and duck hunting or fishing in nearby streams with moderate to good success.

The Yanks found fish, birds, and animals here on the northwest coast that were also common to the

"WINTER QUARTERS" BY GEORGE DAVIDSON COURTESY OF THE OREGON HISTORICAL SOCIETY, NEG #OHS59298

THE COMMANDER ORDERED THE LADY WASHINGTON, A SINGLE MASTED SLOOP, MODIFIED INTO A TWO MASTED SQUARE-RIGGED BRIG. WORK WAS BEGUN AND SPARS CUT...

east coast. The huge trees, also of familiar kinds, clothed the steep mountains even to the water's edge. The usual wild berries and greens were gathered and eaten, and as communication developed with the natives, a new edible root similar to an onion was discovered.

Christmas, 1788, was stormy, but the men tried to be merry. Robert passed out extra grog and a good serving of venison and duck, bread and molasses, and with plum duff (a raisin pastry) for dessert; they called it a feast. Afterwards, the lads did jigs and reels to a lively fiddle and took turns singing both religious and lusty songs.

Robert took stock of his situation on this round-the-world voyage. The Indians could not go out for furs during the stormy winter months. Work was progressing on the chisels to be used for next summer's trade. Even Kendrick, apparently relieved of the pressure to issue sailing orders, was not causing rows. There was plenty of wood to burn to keep warm and fresh meat and fish for food; and every day Nancy, the pet goat, provided milk for tea.

In mid-January, the call went out, "Fire! Fire on the *Columbia!*" A fire from Kendrick's chimney had burned down through the deck. Hot coals had set fire to the sails stored against the gun powder room. All hands fell to with buckets of icy water to put out the fire and avoid a disaster; but the *Columbia* was badly damaged.

The lad who had won the bet went quietly around filling his poke with his winnings.

NOOTKA INDIANS.

After a time, Haswell and others found they could safely visit the nearby village. The Indians lived in plank dwellings, some as long as 100 ft. These were divided into spaces for families each with a fireplace and access to the single, low door carved in the decorated main entrance center pole. Other support columns and pillars were also covered with animals and imaginary beasts. The visitors found the smoke of the cooking fires, the smell of the dried fish hanging from the rafters, and the fish oil with which all food was basted, combined to make a heavy, unpleasant odor in the dark windowless longhouses.

These native people had two unusual physical characteristics.

Their heads appeared to have been shaped. Their foreheads were very shallow and at a point just above the eyebrows the head slanted sharply back to a point at the crown.

The "Boston men" also noted that both the native men and women walked with great difficulty on shortened misshapen legs. They were unable to straighten their knees and had deformed enlarged ankles and unusually wide flat feet. Perhaps this resulted from the men spending many long hours crouched in their canoes and the women constantly squatting at their tasks in the villages.

The natives wore skins or short garments of woven cedar bark, animal wool, or hair. They did not wear shoes, but a woven cedar bark conical hat was worn to shed the rain. On special occasions, after anointing themselves with fish oil and black and red decoration, they covered the top of their heads with a feather crown of soft down and sang and danced while others beat on the roof with sticks and paddles.

A few of the chiefs were familiar with firearms, but for the most part their favorite weapons were a bow and arrow, a spear, and a stone axe. They fished from two-man canoes, but had other canoes that could carry up to thirty people for war or whaling. The only tools they had to make these sleek, efficient dugouts were a sharp rock, a wooden wedge, and a stone mallet.

Some of the Puritan-bred sailors returned from a visit to the Indian village to talk critically about the sights, sounds and smells of the unwashed natives and their primitive food preparation. Everyone agreed that the natives lived close to nature; outspoken Yanks asserted the natives even lived "with nature" when they observed the usual small parasites crawling in the natives' hair and on their clothing. (Not that many of the sailing vessels did not have minute six-legged stowaways aboard in food and bedding.)

But the more thinking members of the crew began to accept cultural differences. There were those

CHINOOK LONGHOUSE COURTESY OF THE OREGON HISTORICAL SOCIETY, NEG #OIIB 1165

aboard who had admired and traded easily for the woven hats, harpoons or bows and arrows. But it was the smooth, water-tight carved boxes; or the blankets woven from the wool of dogs or mountain sheep, that were the most difficult to obtain. Some of the lads yearned to collect a string of the unusual long slender shells the natives used as money, to take home as a necklace for patiently waiting sweethearts.

One might shudder and criticize some of the native customs and beliefs, but who among the crew

THE INDIANS LIVED IN PLANK DWELLINGS, SOME AS LONG AS 100 FT.

could survive if they were thrown into the forbidding northcoast environment? In truth, the native practices and codes had evolved into a viable society from which the white men were now hoping to draw their fortune.

During the winter months the debate raged on: were these natives cannibals? Offers to sell children taken as captives had occurred, and some of the dried foods offered seemed to be of questionable origins.

SPRING OF 1789 - TRADING -

WHALE HUNTING.

The days were getting longer. The number of barrels of chisels was growing.

The crew was well and strong again. Signs of the dread scurvy had disappeared weeks ago. During breaks in the weather the lads took to wrestling and having foot races on the narrow beach.

With the rebirth of spring, Robert felt a "germ of discovery" growing in his being. Was this voyage really going to be the fulfillment of his secret life-long dream?

The Captain remembered the incredibly electrifying moment when he first saw the Strait of Juan de Fuca.

Now he was being nagged by the notion that four great rivers were flowing out from a central, high point on the North American continent. Robert knew the Mississippi River flowed to the south, and the St. Lawrence River flowed east. Explorers and fur traders were tracing a network of rivers in the north. That left the River of the West waiting to be discovered. He was becoming convinced that somewhere, someone was going to sail into a great waterway that drained the western half of the continent.

Robert resolved to listen, ask questions, and to make very careful notations on his charts.

He wanted to be about fur trading before the Englishmen returned to the coast. So in cold mid-March a supply of chisels was put aboard, and the *Lady Washington* set sail south to trade with the Indians.

Kendrick and the *Columbia Rediviva* remained at Nootka Sound.

The *Lady* hugged the coast, stopping when they

saw the smoke of villages. The Yanks learned they were the first whites to visit some of the coves. Fast running tides and the unfamiliar bottom made for some anxious sailing. The chisels proved to be good trade goods, except in villages where shrewd natives demanded as many as ten chisels for one pelt.

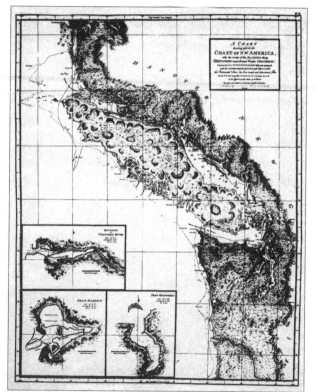

CHART OF THE COAST OF N.W. AMERICA COURTESY OF THE VANCOUVER PUBLIC LIBRARY

THE LADY HUGGED THE COAST, STOPPING WHEN THEY SAW THE SMOKE OF VILLAGES. THE YANKS LEARNED THEY WERE THE FIRST WHITES TO VISIT SOME OF THE COVES.

A side trip into the Strait of Juan de Fuca confirmed it was a large inland body of sea water extending east as far as the eye could see. Gray found it exhilarating to sail into this disputed strait and confirm its existence.

Off the southern entrance to the strait a canoe of fierce appearing natives sold the Yanks some halibut and furs. They seemed to indicate that after a distance the strait branched into two channels, one to the north and one to the south. But was it Robert's intuition, his "sea sense," that made him doubt it was the entrance to a continental passage?

A gale with mountainous seas, followed by continually squally weather, blew the sloop farther south into a familiar cove.

They arrived just in time to join the natives in a whale hunt. The natives' legs may have been misshapen, but their skill and bravery in the whale hunt was greatly admired.

Chief Hanna, of the genteel suit of clothes, and Chief Wickananish invited some of the sloop's officers to join in the fearless pursuit.

The sleek native canoes took them far out in the ocean waves. The pursuers found the whale weakened by the drag of numerous inflated bladders attached to the ingenious harpoons the bold hunters had sent home. The whale dwarfed the fleet of surrounding canoes; one flip of its flukes could have sent them all skyward.

A cheer went up at the final breath from the huge animal. Before it was towed back to the beach, the carcass was decorated with eagle feathers to thank the gods for their bounty.

All the neighboring villages were invited to join in a week-long feast on the whale blubber.

In this harbor the Yanks learned that the natives practiced good basic economics. Chief Wickananish had purchased all the sea otter pelts from the neighboring villages, putting himself in the position of deciding not only the price of all the skins in the area, but also which of the fur traders would be allowed to trade.

When the chisels ran out, Robert hurried back to Nootka Sound. Much to his dismay, during the return trip he found it necessary to pass up about 300 prime skins, due to lack of trade goods.

On entering Nootka Sound they found the Englishman Douglas had returned on the *Iphigenia.* His supply sloop was expected in a day or two.

The *Columbia Rediviva* was still at anchor.

The Spanish - Lob Lip Sound - crash.

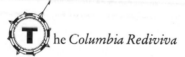 he *Columbia Rediviva* was a hulk. She was not ready for sea. She had not been graved; her hull was still coated with barnacles and marine life which had built up during the voyage from Boston. The gaping black hole from the chimney fire last winter remained.

The blacksmith had been busy making chisels. Robert ordered a large supply put aboard. He instructed the crew to repair the sails and rigging, gather wood and water, and prepare for a voyage to the north immediately.

A week later, in early May, they had hardly lost sight of Nootka Sound, when a Spanish warship fired a warning gun at the *Lady* and ordered the Captain to come aboard. Robert complied. Don Estavan Jose Martinez, Captain of the *Princessa* revealed he was on his way to take command of Nootka Sound. He asked about the vessels there. The Spaniard was cordial to Robert, gave him some brandy and a ham, and then they parted. Robert was decidedly relieved to learn all was well between his country and Spain, as his small sloop would have been no match for the Spanish warship.

As they continued north searching for furs, the Yanks watched for signs of Indian villages. Soon however, canoes laden with furs came off eager to make trades as they had in the past when sails were sighted. The native canoes could skim safely on the shallow water, over the dangerous reefs and sunken rocks; places where the deep-keeled sailing vessels would be wrecked and quickly broken up.

Robert kept the crew busy continuously taking soundings and calling out sightings. He enjoyed the challenge of exploring the gulfs, inlets, sounds, and intricate channels of the broken coast. He attempted to circle lands he believed were islands and watched for notable land forms ashore. His charts were constantly being filled in. Robert took the *Lady* to sea during the heaviest gales, to protect her keel from damage by the reefs, shoals, and rocks on the irregular rugged coast.

Sailing the broken coastline with its strong currents and boisterous weather was a constant hazard. The rigors of plying these unknown waters, close enough to shore to attract the native fur traders, was grueling. Rocks and shoals were an endless danger. The Captain used the skill and experience of his thirty-two years to note the feel and smell of the air, and the direction and intensity of the wind and clouds. He used all his senses in observing the color, currents, swells, and tides of these unknown waters. But more than once, stubborness and just plain good luck helped him secure a safe harbor before nightfall, or as a wicked storm threatened.

One day Robert was drawn away from his charts

by an unusual stir aboard: the approach of canoes carrying men and *women*. It was not common for women to come out, usually only the native men brought furs to trade.

What caused additional commotion among the crew was the sight of the astonishing facial adornment of these women. Their lower lips had been cut to accommodate a decorated wooden disk. These appeared to become larger with the age of the wearer. The largest, about four inches in length, hung down to cover the chin but when these women spoke, it would fly up to cover the wearer's nose.

Even the young sailors eager for feminine companionship, found this custom repulsive. The jokester in the crew named the place, Lob Lip.

Sometimes, in a snug harbor, hard against snow-topped mountains, the crew was able to rest, hunt, and get water and wood. Occasionally, the crew would catch a glimpse of the sea otters also resting on the sheltered kelp beds.

During this time the Yanks gathered information about the sea otter, the small marine mammal whose magnificent, lustrous, black/brown pelts they had been bundling in the hold. The average luxurious skin was about five feet in length, with a skunk-like stripe on its head and a sprinkling of silvery guard-hairs on the shiny rippling coat. A Chinese manda-rin would pay dearly for the twelve-inch tail piece, as the deep thick silky fur was even finer and softer here than in the rest of the pelt.

Traditionally only the chiefs wore sea otter skins. Occasionally a chief would decide to sell his well used royal robe, three sea otter skins pieced together. The traders called these garments taken in trade "coot sacks." Some said the name was derived from the Scottish short garment called a "cutty sark."

In spite of strong currents and reefs, Robert sent the *Lady* through narrow passages and around headlands to discover the outline of the continent, and to set the islands in place. On occasion, power-ful northern tides forced Robert to send a boat ahead with a crew to "man the sweeps," to row and haul the *Lady* away from angry breaking reefs. In bois-terous weather, thick fog, and the eternal rain, the expedition continued in the lengthening northern days.

They entered and named Barrel Sound, Pintard Sound, and Derby Sound for their investors; and labeled the large Washington Island for the great American general, leader of the Revolutionary War.

Three weeks later, as the *Lady* was in the far north at about 55° N and attempting to find a harbor for the night, an icy storm blew up. A heavy gust caught the sails and drove the sloop through a small narrow opening. As the vessel rolled helplessly, her sails and rigging were scraped away by overhanging cliffs. Violent waves crashed over the deck, and then receded to allow the hull to slam on unyielding bedrock. In the steadily increasing wind Robert was forced to order the longboat out to carry an anchor on a long rope attached to the capstan on the vessel. The water-soaked crews bent to the oars, praying they wouldn't be swamped in the heavy seas, and slowly forced the small boat out into the boiling, deep water. They dropped the anchor. The wind whipped the commands out of the mouths of the officers, but the men on deck felt the beat of the chanteys sung in the past, and with the practiced rhythm of doing heavy work in unison, they put their weight and muscle to winding the anchor rope around the capstan on deck. Gradually they pulled the *Lady* away from the shallows and out to the anchor. This desperate operation had to be repeated twice, in frigid seas and wild winds to free the trapped *Lady*.

But she had suffered serious damage to the jibboom and bowsprit. She was a sorry sight with tattered sails and broken rigging as she proceeded slowly south searching for a protected harbor in which to make temporary repairs.

The hand pump was equal to the leak in the battered hull, but for how long? How many weeks would it take to reach Nootka Sound for help with the repairs? Could the weakened vessel withstand more angry storms? The possibility of a shipwreck on the cold bleak coast, rumored to be inhabited by cannibals, was a fate no one dared to mention. In spite of this and in fear that the vessel might break up, Robert held as near to the beach as possible.

A few days after the mishap, Robert and his

gloomy crew were astonished to hear music. They could hardly believe their ears and eyes when a parade of over twenty canoes appeared out of the rain and fog singing a friendly greeting. This warm welcome, and signs that the natives had skins to trade, relieved the American's fear and did much to lift their spirits.

They dropped anchor off the nearby village and trading began, supervised completely by the chief's wife. Again, while it was most unusual for an Indian woman to supervise the trading, it was of great benefit to the Yanks: they purchased 200 prime skins at the unbelievably low exchange of one chisel per pelt.

The next stop was in a sound surrounded by cold, steep mountains, only recently free of snow. The natives here valued iron little, but wisely bartered for clothing. They brought the fur traders halibut and boiled gull's eggs.

At this stop, Robert took no reprisals for the natives' custom of pilfering anything they could. Other traders might have turned their guns on the canoes in retaliation for thefts. That was not Robert's habit, and so in spite of small losses, trade continued uninterrupted until all the available furs were collected.

As Robert carefully guided the *Lady Washington* south, he crossed a large opening that appeared to penetrate far into the continent. Could this be a strait that connected the Atlantic and Pacific?

In 1588 Lorenzo Maldano claimed to have sailed across North America from the Atlantic Ocean into the Pacific Ocean in the Strait of Anian; and, in 1640 Admiral Bartholomew de Fonte gave his name to a strait in the North Pacific he believed to be the western terminus of a continental waterway. Both stories were part of the lore of the sea. Neither man's claim had ever been proven.

Hoping he might at some future time be back to investigate the possibilities, Robert made precise notes on his charts of this wide body of salt water, and other promising gulfs, winding inlets, and unexplored entrances.

Time was his enemy now. He must continue back to Nootka Sound to make repairs.

As they limped south, Robert hoped the gallant

Lady could be made seaworthy in jig time. He was anxious to continue gathering the beautiful warm pelts, while they were still available in exchange for the small chisels. He hoped Kendrick would authorize the *Lady's* repairs quickly and maybe even lend the carpenter of the *Columbia* to help.

Mid-June, almost a month after the crippling crash, the *Lady Washington* finally made Nootka Sound. The Americans were more than a little concerned when they saw two Spanish warships were at anchor in the small harbor and that a small fort flying the Spanish flag had been built to guard the entrance.

But more importantly, why was an English fur trading vessel, here, at anchor, during the best weather?

SPANISH / ENGLISH CONFRONTATION –

SPANISH ACT OF POSSESSION –

CHANGE OF COMMAND.

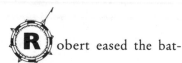**R**obert eased the bat-
tered *Lady* past the threatening cannons on the
Spanish warships and continued in. He dropped
anchor beside the *Columbia Rediviva,* still at anchor
in the protected inland cove.

Shortly, a small boat came off carrying Kendrick
and the Spanish Commander Juan Martinez. They
brought the news that the Spanish had orders to occupy and fortify Nootka Sound in the name of his
August and Catholic Majesty, Carlos III, King of
Spain. The Castillian government had sent Juan

Martinez and the two warships to Nootka Sound to
signify Spanish sovereignty on the Pacific Coast from
Mexico to 60° N, that point where the continental
coastline turns toward The Orient.

Much had happened in this small harbor in the
month-and one-half since the *Lady Washington* had
set out early in May.

Fortunately the Spanish did not appear to have
any territorial problems with the Americans.

As work began on the *Lady,* Robert learned that
the Spanish arrived just days after the *Lady* had sailed.
Kendrick had proclaimed his stay in the harbor was
only temporary. Only then did he begin to work
on refitting and repairing the *Columbia Rediviva.*

Kendrick saw to it that he and Martinez were
soon on the most cordial terms. They began to share
the same cove, workmen, supplies, and tools as
Kendrick repaired the *Columbia* and Martinez, following his orders, began to build a vessel for coastal
exploration.

The Spanish did not know that during the past
winter in Macau, the ambitious fur trader, John
Meares, had devised a plan to control the fur trade

in Northwest America. He had put together a fleet
of four vessels that he was sending to the northwest
coast with the opening of the fur trading season.
Besides his three returning fur-trading vessels, he had
outfitted the large supply ship, the *Argonaut* with
workmen and equipment. It had orders to build a
stronghold to be called "Fort Pitt" at Nootka Sound.
Meares planned to set up a series of smaller perma-
nent trading posts that would exclude all others from
the fur trading area. These would be served by small
coasting vessels to be built at Nootka as needed.

The Englishman's plans were in direct opposi-
tion to the Spaniard's orders. Events during the next
few weeks almost led to war.

Martinez, the naval officer turned diplomat, began negotiations with the strong-willed Capt. Douglas on the *Iphigenia*. He charged this Englishman
on the first Meares' vessel to return to Nootka Sound,
with entering a Spanish port illegally. The confrontation grew from polite inquiries to a heated debate
and finally to the arrest of Douglas and his crew by
Martinez.

At one point, Kendrick agreed to the Spaniard's

request that the *Columbia's* blacksmith make leg irons for the English sailors taken as Spanish prisoners.

After many stormy confrontations and the tedious translations of the Iphigenia's Portuguese sailing papers into Spanish, and Spanish orders into English; only then did Martinez finally allow Douglas to leave Nootka.

But, when Meares' second vessel, the thrifty schooner *Northwest America* arrived, Martinez immediately abandoned his plans to build a small vessel for coastal exploration. He confiscated the English vessel, repaired its wormy planks, and prepared it for a Spanish expedition to the south.

Here again, Kendrick sided with the Spanish. He agreed to hold the ten-man English crew aboard the *Columbia Rediviva.*

After he arrived, Robert grudgingly interrupted supervision of repair work on the *Lady Washington* for the numerous dinners, toasts, and cannon salutes celebrating Spanish religious or political events.

However, everyone willingly stopped work when Martinez invited all nationalities at Nootka Sound to witness the impressive formal act of possession of Nootka Sound for Carlos III, King of Spain. This ceremonial Spanish act was to signify possession and to preserve Nootka Sound from any further foreign encroachment.

On June 24, 1789, when all hands gathered on a prominent knoll, the pomp and ceremony began. Members of the three nations watched attentively as Martinez moved rocks around and slashed at the brush and trees with his sword. No one protested this demonstration of Spain's control and possession of the land. Then at the Spaniard's command, his troops, maintaining solemn military precision, proceeded to erect a large wooden cross. On one side it had lettering honoring Jesus of Nazareth and Carlos III, and on the other side, the years 1774 and 1789, and the Commandant's initials, E.J.M. A bottle containing a witnessed document of possession was sealed and buried nearby.

Not to leave out the testimony of the Native Americans, Martinez called upon Chief Macquinna to give an oral account of the first European flag flown at Nootka. Macquinna carefully described a Spanish naval flag in use in 1774, satisfactorily documenting the prior Spanish discovery.

At the conclusion of the ceremony the Spanish troops at the site fired the usual rifle volley, which was echoed by the thundering guns on the Spanish vessels and at the fort. Martinez declared it a day of celebration and invited the American, British, and Spanish officers aboard his warship *Princessa* for proper toasts of spirits and a sumptuous feast.

As the visitors came aboard, his guests were greeted by rousing cheers sent up by the Spanish seamen, spaced in an orderly fashion in the rigging. Nootka Sound again echoed with booming cannon salutes that followed.

In early July the arrival of Meares' large supply ship, the *Argonaut*, set off another round of charges and counter charges. For two days a loud caustic exchange raged between the two nationals, as Martinez quizzed Captain Colnett regarding his boast that he was a representative of the King of England.

The impasse between the Spanish and the English over the possession of Nootka Sound and the Pacific Northwest, was interrupted by the Americans calling for a proper Fourth of July celebration to mark thirteen years of American Independence.

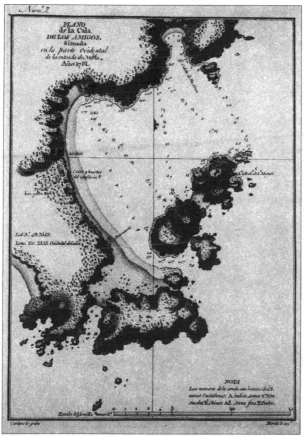

SPANISH MAP OF FRIENDLY COVE COURTESY OF THE VANCOUVER PUBLIC LIBRARY

THEY HAD HARDLY LOST SIGHT OF NOOTKA SOUND, WHEN A SPANISH WARSHIP FIRED A WARNING GUN AT THE LADY AND ORDERED THE CAPTAIN TO COME ABOARD.

The Americans gave their crews the day off. They cheered the Stars and Bars and if they had known that only a few weeks earlier, on April 30, 1789, George Washington had taken the oath of office as President of the United States, they would have cheered even louder. The occasion and the free time gave the Yanks an opportunity to think about how the folks at home were marking the day. It would soon be two years since this crew had sailed out past Boston Light. They fervently hoped to see Boston and family members before another two years passed.

Differences were politely set aside that day during the splendid banquet Kendrick hosted for Spanish, English, and American officers aboard the *Columbia Rediviva*.

The principals, however, could not arrive at a diplomatic solution to the sovereignty struggle on the lonely coast and the international implications of remaining in Nootka Sound were of grave concern to Robert. He wanted to leave before the Americans might be drawn into an exchange of gun fire, and certainly before the arrival of the four-vessel Russian expedition also rumored to be enroute to occupy Nootka in the name of the Russian Tsarina, Catherine II.

In addition, Robert was deeply concerned by Kendrick's collaboration with the Spanish. Kendrick's blacksmith made leg irons to secure the English prisoners for Martinez; at the request of Martinez, Kendrick was still holding the ten English sailors aboard the *Columbia Rediviva;* and finally, when Martinez asked Kendrick to load his guns and train them on the British supply ship, the *Argonaut,* Kendrick obliged.

On July 12, as Martinez was preparing the captive *Argonaut* to sail to San Blas, the third Meares' vessel appeared at Nootka. The Spaniard was able to capture it, the *Princess Royal,* without firing a shot. But he was becoming hard pressed to maintain control of the growing number of stubborn, uncompromising Englishmen he had under guard.

As for the natives, during this time Chief Macquinna was careful not to get involved in the dispute. But on July 13th, his younger brother, Chief Kelekum, became the victim of the prolonged tension in the crowded harbor. Perhaps the English sailors had urged Kelekum to speak up for old friends, the English captains. On that afternoon, as tribal members watched from the shore, Kelekum paddled out close to the Spanish warship and called out that Martinez was dishonest and a thief.

The English seamen knew the meaning of the words and openly enjoyed seeing Martinez the object of this loud and offensive harangue. Martinez tried to ignore the tirade, but upon hearing the translation he lost his patience. The Spaniard felt he was being challenged on every side, his authority questioned, his judgement disputed, and now this painted savage was making him the laughing stock of the harbor.

Martinez, taking aim with his rifle, silenced the antagonistic native with a single shot.

This tragic incident only added to Robert's anxiety.

Now it was the middle of summer. Both American vessels had been repaired and water and wood had been stowed. Even the last of the coaster's skins had been inventoried and loaded aboard the

Columbia. Food supplies for the upcoming voyage had been brought aboard. Robert was impatient to continue fur trading.

Finally, the enigmatic Kendrick made a decision. Making no explanation, he announced a change of command. Robert was given command of the *Columbia Rediviva* with orders to sail to the Orient.

Kendrick apparently was willing to ingratiate himself with the Spanish by holding the ten English sailors aboard the *Columbia,* but he was unwilling to sail to Macau and explain to the international world the reasons for his decision. He transferred command to Gray.

Robert spent no time thinking about Kendrick's reasons. Now was the time to hope the fur market would be up and the voyage profitable. He rejoiced in the wonderful news and quickly ordered his sea chest, logs, charts and maps, and his personal effects aboard the *Columbia Rediviva.*

He reasoned that rank has its privileges and ordered that every comfort be provided for Nancy. The crew willingly joined in the project. She was soon brought aboard to a clean, refurbished stall, complete with a flowery sign over the feed box reading "Nancy's Bower."

The Englishmen's tales of the warmth and splendor of the mid-Pacific islands again filled the crew with anticipation. All aboard anxiously waited for the chance to compare these islands, sometimes called Owhyhee, with the well-known Atlantic West Indies.

HAWAII - MACAU - AROUND AFRICA -

1790 BACK IN BOSTON -

SETTING OUT AGAIN.

The names of the two vessels on the American expedition were chosen with care. The *Lady Washington,* the ninety-ton sloop, was named for the great American general who had held the country to its victorious course. And now, Robert was in command of the larger two-hundred-ton brig, the *Columbia Rediviva,* meaning "Columbia Reborn." Columbia was the name symbolic of liberty and patriotism that was used during the revolution to signify the break with England and the desire for independence in the New World. The name spoke to the emotions of the Yanks and inspired Robert and the crew to continue the voyage.

The Captain was happy for the uninterrupted weeks of sailing into the setting sun. Every croak and groan of the planking sent a message of dependability or risk, and with every squeal and squall of the rigging, Robert was either reassured or alerted to danger. Gray enjoyed the movement of the vessel under his feet. He relished the challenge of watching the rolling sea and reading its briny secrets.

Looking back, he judged his relations and trading with the Northwest natives had been reasonably harmonious, except for the one tragic incident at Murderers' Harbor. Perhaps the natives there had looked on the Yanks as white invaders.

As for the "germ of discovery," Robert felt the season for gathering furs was very short and the keen competition among the fur trading vessels did not give him time for explorations or excursions. He had been able to note an occasional snowy peak on the maps but the fog and rain had made detailed observations of inland prominences almost impossible.

However, pursuing the possibility of a large inland waterway, Robert had questioned the Indians.
The answer was always the same: only mountains
to the east. His careful scrutiny of their tools, jew-
elry, and trade goods also convinced him that these
mountains probably prevented trade with the inland
tribes.

After about four weeks of sailing, all hands were
enjoying the warmth, the food, and the friendly natives of the Hawaiian Islands. Faring better than the
English explorer Cook who was killed here in 1779,
Robert took on water and a plentiful food supply
before setting sail once more.

Here, Robert yielded to the pleas of two young
natives "to see the world." He took Attoo and Opie
aboard.

Late November, 1789 found the Captain and crew
awash in the colorful sites, exotic sounds, and strange
smells of the crowded oriental port of Macau.

As soon as the *Columbia* anchored, the English
crewmen taken captive off Meares' *Northwest
America* hurried ashore to make their report to the

owner. Robert had no doubt Meares' loud outrage and his every complaint would very soon echo about in the highest halls of the King's court in London.

This confrontation between the Spanish and the English on the lonely northwest coast became known as the Nootka Sound Incident.

The Americans had been warned of strange regulations, unending delays, and of the skillful pilfering by the Asians. Now they found the warnings had not been exaggerated.

But, they could not move. They had orders to wait for the *Lady Washington*. She would be bringing additional furs to add to the season's sale.

Near the place where the *Columbia* was anchored, the Boston men discovered a peaceful dockside temple. Here in the quiet they watched politely as the people climbed the steps to place burning incense, as an offering at the ancient yellow and blue temple. A Chinese tradition told of how a young girl, A-Ma, had rescued the crew of a small fishing boat as it was about to be swamped in one of the vicious hurricanes of the South China Sea. The girl appeared in the turbulent waters, swam to the men, brought them ashore, and then disappeared.

When the fishermen found they were unable to find her and thank her personally, they believed she might be a goddess. They decided to build a beautiful pagoda in her honor, and placed it near the harbor looking out to sea. For hundreds of years Chinese seamen and their families had continued to climb the traditional series of steps and platforms to the sacred shrine in honor of the youthful lifesaver. They thanked her for a successful voyage and asked for her continued protection.

While the American seamen's Puritan beliefs were shocked at the worship of a stone goddess, they admired the devotion and sincerity of the worshippers. The men learned that over the years the young girl's name, A-Ma, added to the Portuguese word *cau* for harbor, eventually gave the area the name Macau.

After some time, the Chinese gave the *Columbia* permission to sell her furs.

There was no sign of Kendrick's arrival. The *Columbia* waited. Robert began to hope that soon he would no longer be under the command of the insufferable, dawdling Kendrick.

If "Nimble Jack" did not arrive, Robert would then be free to take the *Columbia* back to Boston.

Finally, late in January, 1790, Robert learned that Kendrick, upon his arrival in another Oriental port, had sold his furs independently. This left the *Columbia* in Canton without sufficient funds to purchase a full cargo of tea and other exotic goods necessary to make the voyage profitable.

Troubled by these obvious financial problems, but carefully keeping copies of all correspondence to and from Kendrick, and accounts of expenses, for explanation to the owners; Robert purchased what he could.

At last, on February 12, 1790, the *Columbia* and crew set out, continuing to chase the setting sun, on the last leg of the around-the-world voyage.

At sea Robert roamed the ship with a sharp eye, keeping her fit and the men at making rigging and the ever constant repairs. His days and nights on the bridge were spent in the never-ending dance with the winds and currents, cautiously moving his vessel with the forces of nature to skillfully guide her safely over the waves.

Robert took the well-traveled route south through the China Sea and the Strait of Sunda, between the islands of Sumatra and Java, into the Indian Ocean. Did the Americans miraculously avoid the attack by the Malaysian pirates? Or could these Persian sea robbers' practiced eye readily see that the American craft was not bulging with gold, silk, and spices? Whatever the reason, Robert and his vigilant crew relaxed as they watched the proas, their sleek swift vessels with their high flying single triangular sail, disappear over the horizon.

The Yanks were able to take advantage of the South Equatorial Current which brought them to the coast of Africa.

As they rounded Cape Horn, the southern tip of that continent in moderate weather, they were reminded of the frigid passage around South America. One of the crew members remembered Kendrick had taken them so far south at that time, he wondered if their round-the-world voyage was to be north to south, rather than west to east.

August 11, 1790: the gypsies of the deep returned to port.

A jubilant Captain Robert Gray sailed the merchant ship, the *Columbia Rediviva,* back into Boston Harbor. He was in command of the first American vessel to sail around the world flying the American flag.

Many a federal salute had been fired by the *Columbia* since she had set sail almost three years earlier, but the thirteen gun salute, with which she greeted Boston to announce her return, had a special sound.

Boston looked warm and inviting to the men on deck. Their eyes filled with tears as they thought of the loved ones they hoped they would soon see.

The long voyage had taken its toll. Gray's face was lined, his clothes hung from a thin frame. It was in a voice heavy with emotion that the Captain had given the command, "Salute." But the crew was in full voice at the end of the charge. Their voices rang out over the water! They danced about, shook hands, and slapped each other on the back. The church bells began to ring and mingle with the cheers and salutes from the crowd ashore.

The Captain and crew were swept up in a day-long celebration. Even Governor John Hancock demanded to meet with the returning officers.

The misery and toil of the long trip were forgotten in the joyous welcome and festivities. Attoo, the Sandwich Island boy, added to the occasion by parading in his colorful feathered helmet and flowing cloak decorated with a design of a brilliant setting sun.

Those on the dock had a good laugh watching Nancy, the goat, trying to walk on her "sea legs."

Because of delays, inexperience, and Kendrick's suspected embezzlement, the voyage had not been profitable. Two of the owners withdrew, but were quickly replaced. Robert was sure he could command a financially rewarding fur trade venture; he willingly invested some of his money in shares to finance a second voyage.

In the past, Boston vessels had easily sailed to

the Orient around Africa. These merchants had met with great success in disposing of the eagerly sought Oriental goods they brought back.

Gray's successful voyage had shown that furs could be a viable cargo for the Canton trade, which would bring new vigor to Boston as a seaport and social center. Many New England shipowners followed up on Gray's success and began immediately to outfit their vessels for the shorter trip around the Horn to enter the fur trade.

The *Columbia's* new owners quickly ordered repairs and outfitting. They took Robert's advice and purchased copper, iron, and blue cloth to trade for furs. Knives, beads, fishhooks, clothing, and buttons were ordered to trade for fresh greens, fish, and game.

As it was much more convenient, the Boston carpenters were ordered to build a keel and some framework for a coastal fur trading vessel to be completed in the northwest. These were stowed aboard the *Columbia.*

After the public welcome and celebration in

Boston had subsided and the refitting was progressing smoothly, Robert took time to renew family ties in his home town of Tiverton, Rhode Island. His father had been dead for many years, but his mother joyfully welcomed her son home again from the sea. The days passed all too quickly, Robert found, as he visited with older brothers and sisters Phoebe, John, Lydia, William, Mary, Isaac, and baby sister Susannah. Robert visited the seven families in turn. He admired the new nieces and nephews that had arrived in his absence and regaled the families with tales of his frightening adventures while being treated to the choicest of produce from garden and pen. Soon the bountiful meals, always topped off with Robert's favorite, either Indian pudding or Apple Brown Betty, made his new wardrobe feel snug.

He returned to Boston to find the *Columbia* in good order.

An anxious crew of thirty young men, mostly in their late teens or early twenties were signed on. As the green-hands worked to put the stores aboard, the weathered seamen sternly cautioned the lads against shipboard profanity or lying. They also retold the ancient legends of sailors sighting serpents and demons far out to sea, and warned of the frightening phenomenon of violent hurricane winds blowing up if ever a sailor began to whistle while aboard.

In spite of the well-known dangers, the eager crew worked with a will to stow beef, pork, flour, rice, peas, and beans enough for four years and dreamed of finding riches in far-off unexplored lands.

Attoo returned Nancy again to her freshened stall.

Robert gathered the usual papers: authorization from the harbor master, the vessel's cargo listing, and the manifest. To these he added a letter of instruction from Joseph Barrell and the owners, and a letter of good wishes from John Hancock, then Governor of the Commonwealth of Massachusetts.

As the Commander of an around-the-world expedition involved in international trade, Robert Gray also proudly carried a sea letter of authorization and approval written by Thomas Jefferson, the Secretary of State, and signed by George Washington, the President of the United States.

On September 28, 1790 six short weeks after docking, the *Columbia Rediviva* again set sail for the North Pacific. She rode low in the water, loaded with supplies for a long voyage.

ST. ELMO'S FIRE - FALKLANDS -
CLAYOQUOT SOUND -
ATTOO DESERTS.

Off the coast of South America, near a region called Patagonia, the *Columbia's* young crew passed their first test in obeying the Captain's orders in an emergency. Land, presumed to be a cape, was sighted. At the same time the vessel's clearance quickly shrunk from 60 to 45 fathoms of water.

The weather grew stormy and dark. Lightning burned a bright zigzag in the inky sky, followed by the crash and rumbling of thunder in the massive overhanging clouds. Soundings continued to indicate the ship was being driven alarmingly close to shore. Robert ordered a halt to the soundings to lessen the crew's fear, and hoping to round the headland, ordered the vessel to turn south and east. As the storm picked up the captain found the ship was being driven against another shore. Realizing they were caught in a wide bay, Robert ordered the crew to strike the sails. The frightened young sailors struggled up the slick, water-soaked rigging and in the howling wind fought the massive sails into tight furls.

From noon until midnight the *Columbia* rode on her anchor. Finally, about two in the morning, the gale abated. The anchor had held. They had not struck bottom, but they were in only 12 fathoms of water. Daylight brought a light breeze. The sails were unfurled and the *Columbia* sailed eastward out of the pocket. The crew had courageously followed Robert's commands and his calm and competence had brought them all safely into the open sea.

The crew argued for some time about who did or did not see "St. Elmo's Fire." There were those who said the eerie glow in the top mast preceded the storm and those who said it enveloped the yardarms in the midst of the storm.

Some were unbelieving. "Corposant? Body of a saint?" they scoffed. Others kept quiet, fearing bad luck for the voyage because of their unbelief.

"How many lights did you see?" one asked.

"We want St. Elmo to have his heavenly mates standing by," another responded, "the more lights the better."

"Did you hear the crackling sound? It made the hair on m'head raise up," one tar commented shakily.

"I heard the fizz and sputter and I could smell the burning. Was that fire and brimstone from hell?" another young sailor wanted to know.

Robert had heard of the parlour games they were playing at home with something they called "electricity." He kept his counsel; he knew they were only a plank away from eternity.

All agreed, as the glow faded away, the flames of fire had *not* moved menacingly *down* the mast; good fortune was predicted this time.

They made the Falklands on January 22, 1791, where they spent eleven long "summer days" of the Southern Hemisphere, overhauling the ship, watering, and hunting. The crew was well, but everyone fortified themselves by eating wild celery and greens to ward off an attack of scurvy. In weather too inclement to set sail, Robert showed the crew where and how to hunt wild hogs in the sand dunes.

There had been sleepless nights when Robert recalled his first rounding of Cape Horn; the silent threatening icebergs and the sixty-foot "greybeards" that crashed across the deck. But this time staying farther north, and blessed with surprisingly moderate weather, the *Columbia* halved the usually wicked passage in the remarkable time of slightly less than a month.

Robert continued to hurry the ship north as he was eager to get his share of sea otter skins during the spring and summer fur gathering season.

Late in April, the cook spread a sack of rice to dry on the warm equatorial deck. Somehow, Nancy slipped her tether and had eaten most of the rice before Attoo discovered her. She soon became desperately ill. One of the crew diagnosed that the rice had swelled in her belly. Regretfully, she succumbed to an overdose of rice, just days short of crossing the equator for the sixth time.

Attoo had the unpleasant chore of telling Robert she had died. Members of the crew would miss her entertaining balancing acts, frolicking about the deck, and the spontaneous vigorous tussels with her that relieved the daily tedium.

All hands gathered on the deck and watched the rays of the setting sun hanging low in the western sky, as Nancy, the gallant sailor and mate, was given to the sea. Now there would be no milk with tea.

As the vessel pressed on, scurvy began to attack the crew. Some of the first stricken, those with the putrid breath and who were unable to eat because of loose teeth and swollen mouth and gums, were rapidly progressing to the second stage with puffy, ulcerated legs.

Robert anxiously pushed the *Columbia* up the coast and finally landed at familiar Hancock's Harbor in Clayoquot Sound on June 5, 1791.

THE "COLUMBIA REDIVIVA" BY DALE HART

His first concern was care for the sick crewmen. Those in the most advanced stages with the ugly bloated legs were carried ashore and buried up to their hips in the sandy soil of the beach. The rest of the crew were sent to gather the greens: wild parsley, hog weed, and a chive-like root for their sick mates and for themselves.

Fresh meat, greens, exercise ashore, and the bitter tea made from young spruce boughs, aided in the speedy and complete recovery of all hands.

Old friends: Chief Hanna, his son Wickananish,

ROBERT WAS IN COMMAND OF THE COLUMBIA REDIVIVA, MEANING "COLUMBIA REBORN."

and brother Tootiscoosettle, welcomed the "Boston men" with wild game and fish when they moved to Friendly Cove in Nootka Sound. The natives updated Robert on the Spanish activity in the area and reported many British and American fur trading vessels around.

Fortunately, there was no news of Spain and England at war.

The Indians' account of the atrocities dealt to them by the whites explained the hostile, well-armed appearance of many of the natives. Fearful of an act of revenge against his party, Robert ordered a careful watch at all times, and directed shore parties to be well armed and ready.

He repeated the warning to the crew that they would have to be constantly on guard to protect tools, equipment, and clothing, as he would order no reprisals for the natives' habit of pilfering.

News of the lively competition he would be facing in gathering furs, persuaded Robert to delay building the sloop. He ordered preparations to enter the trade immediately.

A scant two weeks after making land, and as they

were in the final stages for departure, Attoo was discovered missing. It appeared he had deserted. Robert was furious at the natives who obviously enticed him ashore and at Attoo for participating in their scheme.

Attoo was a foolish lad who did not know the story of Dr. John McKay. The adventurous surgeon had come to the Northwest with Captain James Strange on an East India Company vessel. The captain persuaded the willing doctor to take up residence for the winter of 1786-87 at Nootka Sound with friendly Chief Macquinna.

McKay was to minister to the natives and exclude other fur traders. He agreed to acquire and hold the tribe's furs until the return of the Company's vessel the following spring.

As the winter wore on, the foolhardy doctor found he had the status of neither slave nor tribal member.

Food, clothing, and housing were provided on a whim. The pathetic surgeon was not adept nor equipped to wrest his needs from the land and sea.

The account that circulated of the scrawny, dirty,

vermin-infested, "coot-sack" clad, shoeless, starving white man who begged permission to come aboard the first European vessel that entered Nootka Sound the next spring, was pitiful enough to discourage most sailors who toyed with the idea of experiencing the adventure of living the care-free semi-nomadic life of the Northwest's Noble Savages. Even the allure of smiling dark eyes to a lonesome lad, could not overcome the enormous culture clash.

The American party realized the formerly friendly natives and charming singing Indian maidens were noticeably absent, as well as Attoo. Therefore, when Chief Tootiscoosettle came near, Robert persuaded him to come aboard. Robert immediately took the Chief prisoner and sent his native servant with the message that the Chief would be released when Attoo was returned.

The hostage scheme worked. The Sandwich Island boy was soon returned to the vessel, but the imprisonment of Tootiscoosettle had dealt his dignity a lasting injury.

The Captain had to maintain the respect of the

crew. They knew he was a dedicated man, bent on completing a successful voyage. Even though he would have gladly let the chain of events end there, the seriousness of the desertion demanded punishment. He ordered Attoo flogged in the presence of Tootiscoosettle. Robert further threatened the same punishment for any native who lured any crew member to leave his vessel in the future.

SEA OTTER - AUGUST, 1791 MASSACRE COVE.

The "Boston men" found the fish all recognizable; similar to those on the east coast. But the playful beautiful marine mammal, the sea otter, was unique to the Pacific. It was being sought for its fine, soft fur, recognized world-wide as vastly superior to other pelts. The thick, rudder-like tail and webbed feet were used to pursue fish, its food. The tail piece was sold separately, as this section of shiny soft black fur was more valuable.

The Indians in their shallow draft canoes did not find the sea otter difficult to catch as the family pods lived in the numerous rocky inlets, resting or play-ing on the kelp beds. The female could often be found lying on her back as she suckled her pups, usually a litter of three or four.

The crew members were dubious, however, of the natives' description of the sea otter floating on its back, using his front feet to strike a rock and mollusk together to break open the hard shell to get at the food inside.

The Gray party found that the desired trade goods (copper, iron, and cloth), brought brisk fur trading business. Beads and fishhooks were welcomed in exchange for fresh food.

Robert named a particularly pleasant sound in Chickleset Bay, Bullfinch Sound, in honor of the Boston physician and friend, Dr. Thomas Bullfinch. A crew sent ashore here for wood and water were treated well when they took refuge from a sudden squall in a small native village. The party felt they were the first whites to visit the settlement, but ad-visedly made a short stay.

Early July found Robert trading with the famil-

iar Lob Lip natives in Barrel Sound. John Boit, a
young mate aboard, astounded at the labret, or lip
ornament, the native women were wearing observed
later in wide-eyed wonder, "Some of their lips boom
out two inches from the chin."

Robert jokingly asked Boit for a written testi-
monial to give to his brother Isaac to convince him
of this incredible custom at Lob Lip Sound.

Here again, stories of white traders insulting,
abusing, and disgracing chiefs were told. The natives appeared distrustful of the whites. They were
always armed with a double-ended dagger tied to the
wrist with a thong, as well as the customary bows,
arrows, and spears.

The Yanks continued north, trading for furs when
possible.

While in a cove making repairs, Robert reluctantly gave permission for a three man fishing party
to take the jolly boat to a secluded cove. When it
was time for the boat to return, the signal was fired
but to no avail. A second and third signal also produced no results. A search party was ordered. The
crew was shocked to see it return, towing the jolly

boat, its colors at half-mast. Caswell, the second mate, lay stabbed, stripped, and dead in the bottom. The rescue party reported the body of sailor Barnes could not be retrieved from where it lay some distance from the shore, and they further reported nothing was seen of Folger, the third man.

Robert was stunned.

"Three men!"

"What was the offense?"

"And to whom?"

Taking leave of the dreadful place, now named Massacre Harbor, Robert sought a sheltered cove where he conducted an impressive, solemn funeral and Caswell's body was buried with appropriate dignity.

As the season progressed, chance meetings with American vessels provided Robert with details of violence and murders in the Hawaiian Islands; of a vigorous attempt by Northwest Natives to forcibly take a long boat as it was being launched; and confrontations where whites had killed natives.

Mid-summer at Tatooch: Robert noted that when powerful Chief Tootiscoosettle appeared, immediately the fur trade dried up. Apparently the Chief's pride had not healed in the three months since he suffered the indignity of being taken hostage to free the runaway Attoo.

1791 AND 1792 WINTER AT CLAYOQUOT -

BUILDING THE ADVENTURE.

As the days grew short and the temperatures began to fall, Robert became convinced that the natives would retain whatever furs they had for winter. Mid-September found the *Columbia* and crew back in Clayoquot.

Before the *Columbia* left Boston, it had been agreed that Chief Mate Robert Haswell would be given command of the small sloop, to be built in the northwest for coastal trading.

Haswell selected a sheltered cove at Clayoquot. The keel and framework were removed from the

Columbia and work began on the vessel, the *Adventure*. Close by were plenty of tall straight trees. Haswell, measuring in six-foot fathoms, reckoned many of them were "four fathoms around."

Robert tolerated his former commander, John Kendrick, already at Clayoquot on the *Lady Washington*. Robert had no orders to interfere in Kendrick's use or misuse of the *Lady Washington*. He had no orders to demand an accounting of Kendrick's time and trading.

Some of the captains had gathered about 700 skins in a season. Was Kendrick boasting when he said he had 1200 skins aboard now? "If Cap'n Jack had been even somewhat nimble," Robert thought, "this could be his fourth voyage to China to sell furs." The owners of the *Lady Washington* would probably appreciate an accounting from Kendrick regarding their vessel and his finances.

Within a few days Kendrick sailed for China. He did not give the *Columbia* any letters or messages to take home.

Ashore at the cove, Haswell and a crew of carpenters, sawyers, the smith, and other seamen began work on a small log house called "Fort Defiance."

The crew, glad to be away from the venemous insect stings of the north, enjoyed the time ashore and fell to work with a will.

The prospect of a new assignment, when the sloop would be finished, fired the crew with enthusiasm for the ship-building project. In less than a month a well-built, well-armed shop, and dwelling were occupied ashore, and framing of the sloop was completed. Careful workmanship was a source of pride to this group. Carpenter "Chips" Yendell directed the sawyer and the crew in precise fittings for the small vessel. George Davidson, talented artist sailing as the ship's painter, was planning to add his artistic flair to the finished vessel.

Chief Wickananish and a few natives from the almost deserted village of Opitsatah visited regularly, bringing furs and food to assure their welcome.

The natives noted with amazement the progress being made on the coaster.

Robert ordered a careful watch maintained on the ship and shore. Crews were well armed also while hunting, wooding, and fishing.

The natives' clothes, food, customs, and villages had not changed much since Robert's first visit to the coast. However, some of the Chiefs now wore blankets or coats and many of them were equipped with muskets. Regretfully, signs of small pox and other diseases were present as evidence of the white men's visits.

During the dark and stormy days of winter, Robert would grant the lighting of the smoking lamp aboard. It gave the crew the permission and the flame to light their pipes. Hand work and small repairs were the order of the day.

The crew never seemed to tire of recounting the frightening, yet humorous, experience of the past summer when they were caught in the middle of a tribal territorial rights dispute.

Howls and guffaws below deck would indicate the crew was re-enacting the Clinokah affair.

Clinokah was a wise Haida chief anxious to take

advantage of the white man's ways. Since his village was far from the deep-keeled route of the open sea used by the fur traders, and could only be reached through an intricate passage, he sent his canoes in search of the traders.

One evening a large canoe appeared, its ten occupants singing a friendly greeting. They proposed to lead the *Columbia* to a large store of furs in their village. Since they were weary from long hours paddling in search of a trading vessel, Robert gave them permission to spend the night aboard.

The next day in the usual bad weather, tediously careful soundings made passage through the inlets to their village slow, but eventually it was made and brisk trading began.

The weather moderated and it was peaceful inside the small harbor. Trading continued and some of the *Columbia's* crew elected to go fishing.

Suddenly, Chief Clinokah and his braves on the *Columbia* sighted a large canoe entering the sound. The Chief became extremely alarmed, running about on deck, shouting to his people ashore to come to his defense, and begging Robert to fire on the approaching canoe as they were "coming to kill him." The braves aboard immediately dispersed themselves about the deck, some whooping and brandishing their knives and daggers, others hanging over the rails shouting threats and insults, and daring the intruders to attack.

Crew members with a good ear for languages, would humorously reproduce both the panic and disdain the Haida alternately voiced.

There was no humor in the incident at the time though. Robert, anxious for fear more canoes might be approaching, armed the guns and called the fishing party back aboard.

He ordered the natives ashore. The Haida all left except Chief Clinokah and one brave who refused to leave the ship.

This dilemma was solved when Robert observed to his relief, that the strange canoe did likewise; its warriors were put ashore, then the canoe continued to advance, and the presumed Chief, unarmed, standing up and singing.

As he neared loud shouting broke out, accusations were obviously being exchanged between the two principals. Even without a knowledge of the language, it was clear vehement charges of past offenses and outright treachery were hurled back and forth. Once the grievances were aired, a truce was proposed.

The newly arrived Chief went to the beach and soon returned with all his warriors in his canoe.

Clinokah called his people out to conference. He joined his braves in his canoe. And the confrontation began anew.

The Yanks watched closely as noisy spokesmen in each canoe continued to bawl out charges but all the while each tribe's team of negotiators held whispered conferences.

Finally the two Chiefs took command, stood up, and spoke. An armistice had been struck. The visitors began to pass out liberal servings of dried fish; grunts and lip-smacking testifying to its delicacy. And then the strangers offered dessert. They provided spoon-like utensils for raspberries liberally basted with fish oil.

At the end of the feast, Clinokah cordially introduced Robert to the recent arrival, a Tlinget Chief.

The Chiefs were invited aboard the *Columbia* to trade. Clinokah acted as interpreter and advocate for the Tlinget Chief in the sale of his furs.

Later, the Tlinget Chief explained casually to Robert, that the discussions concerned the boundaries between Haida and Tlinget territory.

The little pageant would conclude with crew members imitating the farewell song the Tlingets sang as they paddled away.

December 25, 1791, Robert ordered Christmas to be kept with as much festivity as possible. The ship and the fort were decorated with fir and spruce boughs. Roast goose, duck, and teal, washed down with generous rations of grog, warmed the spirits and bodies of all hands. Chief Wickananish and his chiefs accepted Robert's invitation to spend the day and dine aboard the *Columbia*.

The twelve noon federal salute honoring the Thirteen Colonies mingled with the sound of the wind and rain in the trees. For a moment, in the silence of its echo, the crew was hushed as each one thought of home and loved ones so far away.

At the New Year, Robert wondered if the adventuresome spirit in him was waning. He pondered the rest of his life.

How many more times around the world? More than once he had risked life, limb, crew, and cargo.

Fortunately his judgement of the flare and sound of the waves in the shallows near shore had been sound.

So far the *Columbia* had cleared the rocks and withstood the gales and the strain of coastal maneuvers in the fog and rain.

He'd been away from home for the past five Christamases. He'd be thirty-seven years old on his next birthday, May 10, 1792.

His great "around the world" dream had been realized, accomplished. This gave him profound satisfaction! He knew something of the length and breadth of that vast Pacific Ocean. Now he could add the outline of the Northwest Coast of America and many islands to that world map he had often drawn as a boy on the sandy beach at Tiverton.

But what of the second challenge he had given himself, those many years ago? The still unsolved search for the continental waterway? True, the Strait of Juan de Fuca was there. But even though maps were circulating with the Anian Strait and the Admiral de Fonte Strait on them, not one of the diligent northwest fur traders Robert had spoken to during the summer months, had claimed to have found either strait.

Had the coast to the south been carefully searched?

An early 1600 Spanish report, and another later in 1755 (a sighting credited to the Spanish explorer Bruno Heceta) claimed to have observed an opening near 46° N with a great river emptying into the Pacific there. More recently the English fur trader Meares named a headland in that latitude Cape Disappointment, when he did not sight the long lost river at that location.

Robert agreed with the theory that at some place there would be a western drainage pattern, carrying water down from the "Mountains of Bright Stones," the chain of high snowy peaks believed to rise between the Mississippi River and the Pacific Ocean.

Once more he studied his notes, maps, and charts.

Everything seemed to indicate it might be worth-
while to scour the coast to the south for the mouth
of the River of the West.

FEBRUARY, 1792 INDIAN ATTACK -
LAUNCH OF ADVENTURE - HARDEN'S DEATH -
MARCH, 1792 DESTROYING OPITSATAH.

Throughout the winter in an effort to gain and maintain the friendship of the natives, Robert and the officers of the *Columbia* made many visits to the nearby Indian village of Opitsatah. They were often called upon to minister to sick natives. The Captain gave freely from the powders and poultices in the ship's supply. He shared with the Indians the same skill, methods, and medicine that he practiced on the crew members.

Robert guardedly permitted a continuing parade of curious chiefs to visit the ship and the work site ashore.

In mid-January, when challenged by Chief

Tootiscoosettle to make an overnight visit to Opitsatah, officers Boit and Hoskins found they were respectfully treated. They were fed well and continuously entertained with feats of strength, energetic dancing, and rhythmic singing and drumming.

The two Americans roamed about freely in the village, now grown to number about 2,000. They saw that many of the braves were armed with muskets, and were alarmed by their accuracy at target practice.

When the officers returned from their visit, they discussed with Robert what they had seen. They reported to him that the chiefs had boasted of the young braves' skill at target practice with muskets.

"What was the reason for the large number of Indians in the village?" the officers asked.

More questions: "Was it the moderate winter that was drawing the tribes from their protected winter villages, back to Opitsatah, their summer village?"

"Or was it a fascination with the activity of the 'Boston men?' "

"Why all the curiosity about the launch date of the sloop?"

Questions were soon answered. The crew was galvanized into immediate action when the officers went through the vessel with the news of a horrid conspiracy. Attoo confessed to plotting with the natives to take the ship and murder them all.

Head Chief Wickananish, and his brothers Tootiscoosettle and Tootoocheetticus, had gathered the other chiefs and their warriors together for an ambush and massacre of the Yankee fur traders. They had promised to make Attoo a great tribal chief if he would wet the muskets, knock the priming out of the small arms, and bring all the powder and musket balls he could carry when the attack began. He was to receive a prime sea otter skin for every musket ball he brought.

The attack had been set "perhaps for this very night."

The native reconnaissance had been deviously careful.

The Yanks had made plans to grave the hull of the *Columbia* to rid her of the accumulation of marine growth. She had been moved some distance from the fort, to a spot convenient to board, just a step across from the cove bank. She was unarmed as her cannon and stores had been unloaded to the beach.

Robert quickly ordered a party to begin at dark to quietly warp the *Columbia* back to her position near the fort. Orders were given to strengthen the fort to protect the almost completed sloop.

All arms were made ready.

Stations were given and crews directed to finish graving the vessel during the night, all the while maintaining constant vigilance.

For days Bo'sun Benjamin Harden had been confined to his bed suffering from dysentery. No matter what he ate or drank, his body reduced it to a foul liquid that carried away all his strength and stamina. No coward though, he asked for a pair of loaded pistols so he could shoot any Indian that came below.

The first hoot, warning of an attack, came just as the bottom of the *Columbia* had been scraped and was nearly burnt. Immediately, every man was at his post, armed, and ready, peering into the darkness.

The natives soon discovered their first target, the

Columbia, had been moved. Their cries of dismay echoed across the black water. Some of the crew called to the chiefs by name,

"We're waiting for ya, Tootsee."

"Come on, 'Weak Ann,' we're ready!"
taunting them and daring them to show themselves.

Only hideous whoops and shrieks were returned. The canoes did not enter the cove. Not a shot was fired that night.

A vigilant watch was kept until dawn. No one slept. It appeared the massacre attempt had been thwarted.

Even though the night had been sleepless, work continued all day without a grumble. On the mid-morning tide, work was completed on cleaning the *Columbia's* hull. Restowing began immediately on the cargo and the cannons mounted, to arm her.

A crew was sent with additional lines to secure the sloop *Adventure* as a precaution against the natives stealing or destroying her.

As tools and valuables from the shop were being taken aboard and the cannon ashore made useless, two canoes of lower ranking natives arrived under the pretense of selling fish. But they were actually seeking information.

They asked questions about all the action and future plans. Their questions went unanswered and they were sent brusquely away.

That night the watch heard crashing in the brush nearby and people on the beach; but no assault.

In the morning, as a precaution, Robert ordered several charges of grape shot fired into the beach cover, before the crews went to work ashore.

Late in the morning all work stopped as a canoe was sighted entering the cove. Workers eased towards their arms. The air was heavy with silence and caution as treacherous Chief Tootiscoosettle was seen guiding a canoe carrying himself and his father into the cove. The Chief was attempting a show of friendship but could not conceal his obvious fear. The crew stood silently watchful as Tootiscoosettle produced a few skins he had to sell, and extended a feeble invitation to visit the village.

He would not come aboard but sent the old man with the furs.

All watched as Robert deliberately and contemptuously took the furs and then coldly told Tootiscoosettle to collect for these from his own tribal members who had not returned the musket and coot sack Robert had lent them.

With steely, angry eyes, Robert ordered Tootiscoosettle never to return or he would be instantly shot.

As for penitent Attoo, Robert had to accept the fact that Attoo was not trustworthy. Attoo would fall victim to any scheme that promised him glory or riches. Perhaps that was his motive for joining the American expedition. Hereafter, Attoo would be under constant surveillance and would not be allowed to leave the ship unaccompanied ever.

The next few days the crew, under anxious guard, worked hurriedly to complete the *Adventure*. She was successfully launched February 23, 1792, the first American vessel built on the Pacific Coast. She was about 45 tons, with a handsome figurehead and sleek smooth lines.

Then the small fort ashore was torn down.

As the rigging and outfitting was being completed on the *Adventure,* Benjamin Harden succumbed to his lingering illness. A sombre Captain performed divine services and Harden's remains were buried quietly on shore.

Orders were prepared for Haswell and his crew of ten seamen and tradesmen to cruise to the north on the *Adventure*. Robert and the rest of the crew would take the *Columbia* south. The first rendezvous was set for mid-June.

In the days after thwarting the natives' attack, waves of strong emotions washed over the Americans; intense anger, exploding outrage, and sour disappointment. Each layered between surges of immeasureable relief to have escaped the murderous plot.

When preparations for sailing were nearly complete, Robert went to visit the village Opisatah. He found utensils scattered about and grass beginning to grow in the compound. Tools and clothing had not been taken. It looked as though the village had been hastily abandoned, probably within hours of the unsuccessful attack on Adventure Cove.

There were about two-hundred longhouses here. Over the years, they had been adorned with the tribe's symbolic carvings, both inside and out. The usual entrances were formed from upright logs centering the roof, with the traditional carvings of fish, whales, birds, and animals of the forest parading down to an open mouth doorway.

The sight of the silent village brought back profound feelings of betrayal. After the Americans' many months of kindness and friendship, their sincere efforts to relieve the natives' misery and suffering, the fiendish natives who had lived here, were so unfeeling, ungrateful, as to plot a bloody and vicious death for their benefactors.

These Americans did not practice treachery in their trades. They had always been careful to treat the natives fairly. The traders waited patiently for the natives to show satisfaction before closing a deal. No one could accuse Robert or his crew members of the malicious abusive attacks other whites may have made, blatantly robbing the native.

Robert's last order before he set sail was to direct a crew to destroy Opitsatah, the village that had given shelter to the deceitful tribes. As the *Columbia* sailed out of Adventure Cove, black smoke rose from Opitsatah. The ancient tribal summer refuge was soon enveloped in all-consuming flames, but no one felt the better for it.

APRIL 28, 1792 VANCOUVER AND BROUGHTON –

MAY 7, 1792 GRAY'S HARBOR –

MAY 11, 1792 COLUMBIA'S RIVER.

All during the month of April the *Columbia* scoured the coast, continuing as far as 42° S. Robert observed that this coastal land was more regular than the northern rugged shore-line. Here, high, tree-covered hills came down to narrow strips of flat land that extended to the sandy beaches. He found the coast to the south did not provide many promising harbors.

This was the voyage Robert had dreamed of and had planned for during the past winter months. His "germ of discovery" was swelling in the belief that he was near the Northwest Passage; that he was within range of the River of the West.

Grateful for the reasonable weather and better visibility in which to observe the beach and watch for possible openings, Robert continued to slowly and carefully search every break in the headlands, and to look for signs of a large influx of fresh water entering the Pacific Ocean. Was he investigating the river reported in the early 1600s by the Spanish explorer, Martin de Aguilar?

In general, trading was brisk and many canoes came off bringing furs to trade. The natives continued to accept in trade the small hammered copper pieces which they greatly treasured.

The crew of the *Columbia*, now only twenty men since ten had sailed on the *Adventure*, were happy to continue south past horrid Murderers' Harbor. They knew that four years ago, the natives at that sight had killed Robert's cabin boy.

The Yanks found they could not understand the natives' language at the most southern point of their voyage. At a place the natives seemed to call

"Umpqua," large canoes of particularly fierce-look-
ing natives came off. One of these canoes held up
meat for sale. The Yanks were not familiar with the
dark red meat; they hesitated. To recommend the
food, the natives cut off bloody raw chunks and began to devour them greedily. The Yanks immediately became nauseous as cannibalism came to mind.
The crew was especially glad to sail away from this
terrifying tribe.

Robert ordered his ship to head back north again.

For several days he held the ship off a promising opening at approximately 46° N latitude, at what
he believed to be "Bahía de la Asunción de Neuestra
Señora," the name given to the sighting by the Spaniard
Hezeta on August 15, 1775. The currents and ed-
dies here had proved so strong Hezeta had reported
he was unable to enter and investigate the bay he
believed to be the entrance to a great river or a passage
to another sea.

The same situation prevailed in April, 1792.
Robert also thought the volume of muddy water being
carried out to sea at this point, indicated a sizeable

river. Robert was determined. Since he was not allowed to enter it now, he would return and wait for
the moment when the winds and the tide would permit
him to explore its possibilities.

As he continued north, two British vessels were
sighted: Captain George Vancouver in the *Discovery*
and Lieutenant William Broughton in the tender
Chatham.

They reported they were on a voyage of discovery. The Americans were the first sail they had sighted
since leaving Hawaii eight months ago.

When Vancouver found he had made contact with
the American, Captain Robert Gray, he immediately
sent Lieutenant Puget and the expedition's botanist,
Mr. Menzie, to board the *Columbia* to request further information especially regarding the Strait of Juan
de Fuca.

The English sea captain and fur trader Meares,
in one of his customary tall tales, had spread the false
story in London that Robert Gray had sailed inland
on the Strait of Juan de Fuca, then north through
some islands and ultimately back into the Pacific.

Robert gave the English expedition factual an-
swers to all their questions, denying Meares' story,
and locating the Strait for them — about eight leagues
to the north. Gray told Vancouver he agreed with
those who thought the Strait did not penetrate the
continent to any great distance.

The Americans told Vancouver of standing off
nine days at the mouth of a large river to the south,
waiting for an opportunity to explore it. Vancouver
responded he did not consider that opening worthy
of his attention.

Robert kept a distant surveillance of the Englishmen until he observed them heading into the
Strait.

The *Columbia* again turned south. Robert saw
an inlet which had the appearance of an entrance to
a good harbor. He sent a boat into this uncharted
harbor.

Currents, visibility, and tide cooperated. With
a boat ahead and the mast lookout, the *Columbia*
entered a never-before charted harbor at 46° 58' N.
Gray named it Bullfinch Harbor, for his loyal sup-
porter in Boston, but the crew said it should be called

Gray's Harbor in honor of his discovery. Robert celebrated his thirty-seventh birthday here, May 10, 1792.

Many very well-armed natives came off to inspect this, the first sailing vessel to enter their harbor. Furs and fish were purchased reasonably for blankets and iron. But it was deemed no wooding or watering parties could go ashore safely here.

That night, at the first whoop of the natives, all hands went to their stations. In the bright moonlight, the Yanks could see canoes approaching the ship. Warning shots were fired over their heads. But the Indians continued to advance in spite of forewarning shots. At last the order to fire had to be given and a large canoe with about twenty men in it was destroyed.

The next day trade continued without incident. The natives did not seem to comprehend the noise and death wrought in the night.

Boit, the chronicler, thought the Columbia should stay to gather many more sea otter and beaver furs available here. But Robert wanted some "frosting on his birthday cake."

Robert could not tarry here. He was determined to find that continental waterway. He felt compelled to go that short distance south to 46°10' N. He was certain he would find a large river there.

At high water on the afternoon of May 10th, the ship left Gray's Harbor. She turned south and sailed by moonlight until 4:00 a.m.

No one was asleep. All bets were made.

"The old man will make it!"

"If he can find a harbor that isn't there, he can sure find one that was there for Martin d'Aguilare in 1602 and again for Bruno Hezeta in 1775."

"Let's find that mouth of the River of the West."

"We're going to rename the north headland. Cape Disappointment is what Meares called it in 1788. We're going to prove that lying prevaricator wrong!"

The wind was favorable and it being about half tide, Gray wrote in his log on May 11, 1792:

At eight a.m., being a little to windward of the entrance of the Harbor, bore away, and run in east-north-east between the breakers, having from five to seven fathoms of water. When we were over the bar, we found this to be a large river of fresh water, up which we steered. Many canoes came along side. At 1:00, p.m., came to with a small bower, in ten fathoms, black and white sand. The entrance between the bars bore west-south-west, distant ten miles; the north side of the river a half mile distant from the ship; the south side of the same two and a half miles' distance; a village on the north side of the river west by north, distant three quarters of a mile. Vast numbers of natives came alongside; people employed in pumping the salt water out of our water casks, in order to fill with fresh, while the ship floated in. So ends.

So ends the great search and the great discovery! So ends?

The jubilation of the Captain and the crew called for a federal salute and a round of grog before the "heavy gales and rainy, dirty weather" of the twelfth of May set in.

The American seaman realized a vessel may carry cargo from place to place, but when a captain points

his vessel across uncharted waters and enters a continental waterway heretofore unknown to the outside world, it is an unmatched experience. For years
to come they would be telling their children and
grandchildren of the astounding events of the past
two days.

The *Columbia* spent a leisurely nine days trading, making repairs and exploring the area of the
mouth of the river. On the fourteenth of May, the
ship was able to go twelve to fifteen miles upriver
before grounding.

Trading canoes found them there, some perhaps
from one of the fifty Indian villages reported to be
up the river.

Boit recorded, "The river extended up to the
northeast as far as the eye could reach."

On the fifteenth, Gray, Boit, and Hoskins went
on shore without incident. They hiked around and
found the area was covered with large straight trees
separated by patches of open ground, which seemed
to invite settlers' cabins and gardens.

The sixteenth and seventeenth found the ship

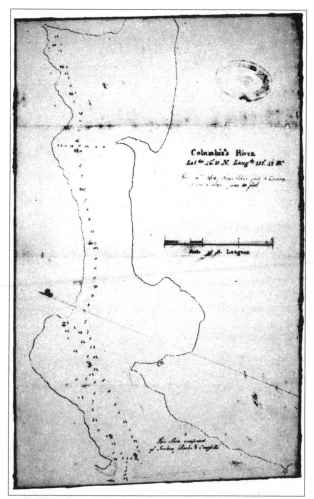

FOR SEVERAL DAYS HE HELD THE SHIP OFF A PROMISING OPENING AT APPROXIMATELY 46° N LATITUDE.

CAPTAIN GRAY'S CHART OF THE MOUTH OF THE COLUMBIA RIVER COURTESY OF THE PUBLIC RECORDS OFFICE-KEW, RICHMOND, SURREY ENGLAND. REFERENCE #MPG557 anchored opposite Chief Polack's north shore village of Chinouk. The ship's tradesmen found trading reasonable; copper and spikes were exchanged for otter, beaver, and other land furs. The beaver furs were hanging about like huge, dark brown flapjacks.

These natives did not have the extreme acquisitiveness of the northern tribes. The expedition suffered no pilfering while in the river.

The shortened crew took advantage of the shelter and worked diligently at the harbor chores of repairing sails and riggings, caulking and painting the ship and the pinnance.

Care was taken in anchoring as the outgoing tide, reinforced by a heavy spring run-off, was powerful. Whole trees were being carried out.

The weather was pleasant. On the eighteenth, Robert eased the ship down to survey the bar to calculate the best time and place to head out. After a good look, he sailed back and anchored opposite the village of Chinouk.

On the nineteenth of May, 1792 it gave Captain Robert Gray of Tiverton, Rhode Island, great satisfaction to note in his log and on his charts that he had named the once fabled River of the West, Columbia's River.

A couplet rang in Robert's ears:

Columbia, Columbia to glory arise,
The Queen of the world and child of the skies.

He remembered the emotions of his youthful Revolutionary days, and the desire for freedom and patriotism the name evoked

During the Revolution, the colonists had given the name Columbia to the new republic, to honor the 15th century explorer who discovered the continent. Columbia was used to represent liberty and patriotism. Pictures depicted Columbia as a beautiful, graceful woman dressed in a flowing gown, wearing a plumed helmet, and carrying a shield covered with thirteen stars. She appeared in news stories, poems, and illustrations. The poetical name continued to be used in oratory and writings calling for unity and support for the young nation.

Further, Robert and his vessel had surpassed the

challenge of the owners and the vessel's glorious name. Together they had brought distinction to the maritime trade of the United States by opening the South American trade route to the lucrative, exotic exchanges with the Orient.

In choosing Columbia for the name of the River of the West, Robert sent a signal to all nations, and especially to the British explorers in the North Pacific at the same time, that the new discovery was directly linked to the fledgling country on the east coast of the continent. Robert's choice of names was almost prophetic. He could not have known that a few months before, President Washington on the Atlantic side of the "sea to sea," had given the name District of Columbia to the Potomac River site he had selected for the capital of the United States.

"It has been three hundred years since Columbus discovered America and less than two hundred years since the Puritans first landed in the New World," Robert thought. "And I, Robert Gray, descendant of the Puritans have carried their dreams of freedom to the western terminus of the American continent."

Gray named the north side of the entrance to the river Cape Hancock for the Governor of Massachusetts. He named the south side Adams Point, not to slight the Vice-President of the United States.

The exploring duly noted and done, May 20, 1792, in a gentle breeze and pleasant weather, on the high tide at 1:00 p.m., Robert took up anchor and headed out over the bar. By 5:00 p.m. the *Columbia* was out and clear, catching the southern breeze which carried them north for more furs and visits with friends to tell of their adventure.

Doing what he knew best, as well as he could, Robert gave his country claim to the watershed of the Columbia River system. He could only guess at its future import.

After leaving the River of the West, the *Columbia* encountered continued native hostility as she sailed north trading for furs. On June 17th, both the *Columbia* and the *Adventure* arrived at the rendezvous safely. However, as they set sail a few days later, the *Columbia* struck a sunken rock and suffered serious damage to her hull. Gray decided it would take a large safe harbor, many hands, and several weeks to make her seaworthy enough for the long voyage home.

He took his vessel to Nootka Sound where Commandante Don Francisco Bodega y Quadra was awaiting his English counterpart, Captain George Vancouver, to negotiate a solution to the Nootka Sound Controversy.

Under the Spanish, Nootka Sound had become an oasis of civilization. They provided fresh food, and assistance with repairs to weary fur traders of all nations. Bodega ordered his men to cooperate with the Americans in every possible way.

Bodega was anxious to purchase the American's handsome sleek sloop, the *Adventure*. In appreciation for his kindness, Gray sold it to him at the end of the fur gathering season for a modest price.

When Vancouver arrived at Nootka Sound in late August, 1792 negotiations between him and Bodega soon reached a deadlock. Both agreed to refer the matter to their superiors and began preparations to leave the cold north coast. On October 19, 1792, as Vancouver headed south, he ordered Lt. William R. Broughton, in the armed tender *Chatham,* to enter Columbia's River. Broughton was able to travel inland for about one hundred miles.

The Americans arrived in Macau to sell their furs in December, 1792. They found the fur market depressed. However, Gray purchased a full cargo of teas, nankeen, a small portion of sugar, and china porcelain.

The *Columbia Rediviva* made Boston on July 25, 1793. Gray had been away for a total of almost six years, except for about six short weeks ashore in Boston between his two voyages around the world.

Robert Gray and Martha Howland Atkins were married February 13, 1794 in Boston and Robert John

Don Quadra Gray was born that fall. In due time he was joined by four sisters.

Captain John Kendrick was accidentally killed in Hawaii on December 17, 1794. A charge mistakenly left in a celebration salute, pierced the hull of his vessel, wounding him fatally.

In 1798 Gray began an ill-fated voyage to the Northwest. He was captured by the French, his vessel seized, and he was held prisoner in Montevideo, South America. In 1799, after his release, he is listed as the captain of the privateer, *Lucy*.

At the end of the hostilities with France, it is believed that Gray generally sailed on coasting vessels, with an occasional trip to England or Europe.

Gray's vessel is recorded at Charlestown, South Carolina, the summer of 1806 — the year of the yellow fever epidemic. Gray died that summer and since no burial site has ever been found, it is believed he was buried at sea. Gray's son Robert died in 1801. Gray was survived by a wife and four daughters.

A Chronology of the American Northwest

16th to 19th Century

1579

Englishman Sir Francis Drake sails along north Pacific to 42° N on Oregon coast.

1592

Report of alleged sighting of Strait of Juan de Fuca.

1603

Spaniard Martin d'Aguilar notes opening between capes on north Oregon coast.

1741

Vitas Bering, Russian expedition, sighted North American continent near present city of Cordova, Alaska.

1744

Spanish navigator Juan Perez reaches 54° 40' N, southeastern Alaska.

1775

Spaniard Bruno de Hezeta turned back at the mouth of great river on Oregon coast.

1778

English explorer Captain James Cook visits Nootka Sound.

1786

French expedition commanded by Jean Francois Galaup, Comte de la Perouse, takes possession of Lituya Bay in southeastern Alaska.

1787

Captains Kendrick and Gray, first American trading expedition leaves Boston for American Northwest.

1789

Nootka Sound Incident.

1790

Captain Robert Gray delivers furs in Canton, returns to Boston; first American on an American vessel to carry the American flag around the world.

1791

Coastal fog prevents renowned Spanish explorer
Alejandro Malaspina from sighting
d'Aguilar-Hezeta river.

1792

Captain Robert Gray enters Gray's Harbor and
the Columbia River.

1803

Louisiana Purchase brings U.S. territory west to the
summit of the Rocky Mountains.

1804

Lewis and Clark Expedition sets out for the mouth of
the Columbia River.

1805

Lewis and Clark arrive at mouth of the Columbia River.

1806

Russian expedition to establish a fort on, and explore, the
Columbia River fails when scurvy forces Juno
to turn back.

1808

Russian schooner SV Nikolai, bringing fur traders and
settlers to the Columbia River, wrecks off
Washington coast.

1811

American fur traders arrive at mouth of Columbia River; build Fort Astoria.

1812

Russians establish Fort Ross in northern California.

1819

Transcontinental treaty with Spain releases Oregon Territory at 42° N.

1824

Treaty with Russia releases land south of 54° 40' N

1846

Treaty between U.S. and Great Britain continues boundary from summit of Rocky Mountains to the Pacific Ocean at 49° N.

1848

Oregon Territory established by Congress.

1859

Oregon statehood.

1889

Washington statehood.

1890

Idaho statehood.

CHRONOLOGY DATA COMPILED
WHILE DOING RESEARCH FOR A BIOGRAPHY OF
CAPTAIN ROBERT GRAY
© 1988 JOEAN K. FRANSEN

THIS BOOK CONTAINS EXCERPTS FROM
THE UNPUBLISHED MANUSCRIPT
"GRAY AND THE U.S.A. FROM SEA TO SEA"
© 1988 JOEAN K. FRANSEN

CAPTAIN GRAY FRONTISPIECE COURTESY OF
THE OREGON HISTORICAL SOCIETY
NEG #OHS586

PRINTED ON ACID FREE PAPER

BOOK DESIGN BY
DALE HART